Digital Marketing Management

Digital Marketing Management

A Handbook for the Current (or Future) CEO

Second Edition

Debra Zahay, PhD
President, Zahay, Inc.
Professor of Marketing,
St. Edward's University, Austin, TX

BUSINESS EXPERT PRESS
Leader in applied, concise business books

Digital Marketing Management: A Handbook for the Current (or Future) CEO

Copyright © Business Expert Press, LLC, 2020.

First published in 2020 by
Business Expert Press, LLC
222 East 46th Street, New York, NY 10017
www.businessexpertpress.com

ISBN-13: 978-1-95152-792-1 (paperback)
ISBN-13: 978-1-95152-793-8 (e-book)

Business Expert Press Digital and Social Media Marketing and Advertising Collection

Collection ISSN: 2333-8822 (print)
Collection ISSN: 2333-8830 (electronic)

Cover image licensed by Ingram Image, StockPhotoSecrets.com
Cover and interior design by S4Carlisle Publishing Services Private Ltd., Chennai, India

Second edition: 2020

10 9 8 7 6 5 4 3 2

Printed in the United States of America.

Dedication

To my husband Edward Blatz, my mother Joyce Zahay and our families, and the late MaryLou Roberts for her guidance and inspiration.

Abstract

This book is for managers and would-be managers who need to upgrade their knowledge of digital marketing. Told from the perspective of marketing strategy, it puts digital marketing in the context of firm strategy selection. The first step in digital marketing is to understand your company and your brand. The next step is to put content and keywords on your website so that they can be found in search. The next step is to use the other delivery platforms of digital content, e-mail, social, and mobile, to deploy that content to the customer. The final topics in the book focus on the importance of data management and privacy. I discuss how to develop a database and an integrated data platform and how to create an organization that puts data quality at its center. These practices are as critical to digital marketing success as the digital marketing delivery platforms. Without quality data, no digital marketing program can be successful. After discussing how to create processes for high-quality data and a platform to manage that data, I then briefly discuss the use of analytics in digital marketing. Finally, I cover issues in managing digital marketing organization in the age of automation. In particular, I examine the skills needed for digital marketing and the best way to structure an organization for knowledge transfer in the area. After reading this book, the reader should have a good idea of where to start on the path to an integrated digital marketing management strategy. Each chapter concludes with a list of action steps or "what to do next" to get started on implementing a digital marketing strategy, as well as review questions and key terminology.

Keywords

Digital marketing; search engine marketing; e-mail marketing; social media marketing; data quality; database management; data analytics

Contents

Acknowledgments

Victoria Crittenden, Rich Hagle, Charlotte Mason, George Milne, Kurt Ruf, Lisa Spiller, Thorne Washington

Introduction

When I began my career as a marketing professional, e-mail was a rare privilege. There were four major forms of marketing communication: in-person, phone, fax, and postal mail. Everything that we needed to know about the customer we learned from talking to the customer, through research surveys, or from transaction records, laboriously collected, and sometimes painstakingly supplemented. There was no online behavioral data to analyze, no web logs, or click-through rates.

I remember, not too long ago, going through hard copies of printouts with a yellow highlighter to pick out the industries which were most likely to yield increased sales in terms of vertical marketing specialization (a technique which worked, by the way). I was somewhat unique in having come from an information systems background and being able to coax decisions from data in the organization. Those who knew how to do so usually labored, as I did, in direct marketing, one of the few areas of marketing which relied on customer data analysis for decision making.

Now I would argue that an individual who is in marketing cannot escape the inexorable rise of technology and its applications. A proliferation of communications channels and a reliance upon technology by both business-to-business (B2B) and business-to-consumer markets (B2C) mean that we marketers are dependent upon the importance of digital marketing. Not only that, digital marketing is the responsibility of everyone in the organization, beginning with upper management. For example, if 93 percent of purchases begin with searching the web, then search is everybody's business in the company, not just that of marketing.[1]

This book is a handbook for the management of digital marketing. It is not, like my other digital marketing book, *Internet Marketing: Integrating Online and Offline Strategies in a Digital Environment*, 4th edition, with MaryLou Roberts, designed to also be used in a skills-based course

---

[1]Sticky Branding. "93% of B2B Purchases Start with Search." https://stickybranding .com/93-of-b2b-purchases-start-with-search/, (accessed October 13, 2019).

and provide a detailed overview of the ins and outs of the execution of digital marketing. Those seeking to learn the details of operating social media platforms or how to effectively create paid search ads can look to that text or other resources to do so.

This book is for managers, students of management, or would-be managers, and those who are just seeking knowledge of the subject who need to know not *how* to do things on digital marketing tools but *why* to do things. The intent of this book is to teach managers how to reframe and rethink their organizations so that digital marketing is integral to their operations. A 2013 study from the Online Marketing Institute said that only 8 percent of brands think that their team is up to speed in digital marketing and strong across all channels.[2] In 2019, Econsultancy published a report with similar results. In this report, only 8 percent of the 500 CMOs interviewed said that there was not a skill gap in marketing.[3] In my classes, I supplement this material with practical, hands-on applications, such as the Google Ad Grants Online Marketing Challenge (OMC) or an Internet marketing simulation.

This book will also help pinpoint the people skills necessary to build the digital marketing organization and also help identify and classify the important elements of digital marketing in the organization. Although there are some leading-edge programs in this area, marketing academics have been slow to make the transition to digital marketing. A recent study by Langan, Cowley, and Nguyen found that only one in ten university undergraduate marketing programs accredited by Association to Advance Collegiate Schools of Business (AACSB) requires a digital marketing course in the core marketing curriculum.[4] Therefore, this book plays an

---

[2]Gesenhues. 2013. "Study: Only 8% of Brand Believe Their Marketing Team Is Strong across All Digital Marketing Channels," *Marketing Land.* https://marketingland .com/study-only-8-of-companies-believe-marketing-team-is-strong-across-all-areas-of-digital-marketing-64404, (accessed November 13, 2019).

[3]Marketing Charts. February 27, 2019. "What Skills Would Marketers Stake Their Future on?" https://www.marketingcharts.com/business-of-marketing/staffing-107533, (accessed October 10, 2019).

[4]R. Langan, S. Cowley, and C. Nguyen. 2019. "The State of Digital Marketing in Academia: An Examination of Marketing Curriculum's Response to Digital Disruption," *Journal of Marketing Education* 41, no. 1, pp. 32-46.

important role in terms of its use in upper-level master's classes and as a resource for managers.

This book is relevant because what constitutes digital marketing is constantly evolving, with skills in data analysis and management, content marketing and storytelling, and the user experience becoming core skills to accompany competencies in search, e-mail, and social media. Increasingly, flexibility and openness to new ideas are just as critical as skill sets in managing a digital marketing team. It is more likely than ever that skills and specializations will have to be developed in-house as well as hired from without, because of the shortage of those with knowledge in this field. Managers need to know what skills and capabilities to develop in their employees, not necessarily have the skills themselves.

To summarize, the book's target is anyone who needs to understand how to incorporate digital marketing into their organization at a strategic level. It is hoped the book will be as useful to the small business owner as to the CMO of a large company. Many of those reading this book developed and succeeded in their careers in an era without Facebook, Twitter, e-mail, and paid search; many are "digital natives" but use the Internet for their own education and enjoyment and not for marketing purposes. The book can be read on its own or to upgrade your skills or as part of an undergraduate or master's level course in the subject.

The book will focus on current technology usage but not the details, which change on a daily, if not hourly, basis. This book is meant, as the title says, to be used as a guideline for the management of digital marketing processes. I hope that, at the end, readers will have a better idea of why these principles and ideas are important and how to implement them in the organization. So, let's get started. . .

PART I

Foundations

CHAPTER 1

How Did We Get Here? Definitions and Background

As you read this book, you will see how to incorporate digital strategy into firm strategy. These key elements of strategy are core competencies, how to produce value, and basic positioning theory. The book then explains to managers how marketing strategy and objectives can be incorporated into the design of a web and mobile site and then through to what I call the four foundations of the digital marketing delivery mix (DMDM) (see Figure 1.1)—search, social, e-mail, and web/mobile.[1] The importance of quality customer data as the foundation for these strategies is also explored here with managerial implications. Finally, guidelines for managing the successful implementation of these marketing technologies in the organization are presented and covered.

It is worth noting how we arrived at the point where digital marketing is now one of the proper occupations of the executive suite. Today marketers are concerned not only about digital marketing but increasingly about the analytics to gauge their effectiveness. However, many companies struggle to staff their organizations with the basic skills needed in critical areas such as content marketing and video production.[2] Although marketing has always been an important and sometimes overlooked occupation in a corporation, digital marketing screams for the attention of not only the chief marketing officer but the chief executive officer as well. A report by ExactTarget

---

[1] D. Zahay-Blatz. 2013. "Four Foundations of the Digital Marketing Mix," *New Interactive Marketing Updates*. http://niuinteractivemarketing.blogspot.com/2014/02/four-foundations-of-digital-marketing.html, (accessed October 13, 2019).

[2] Tom Treanor. 2019. *Digital Marketing 2019: 10 Top Skills Your Digital Marketing Team Needs*. https://blog.treasuredata.com/blog/2019/01/03/the-top-10-digital-marketing-skills-your-team-needs-in-2019, (accessed April 20, 2020).

Figure 1.1 The four foundations of digital marketing delivery mix integrated with marketing strategies and objectives

indicated that marketing priorities have shifted to measurement and data, branding, and online conversion rates.[3] With the exception of branding, most of these terms were not even considered a part of traditional marketing a few years ago. Now, if you can digitize the information, you can measure it. The increased importance of measurement in marketing has paralleled the increase in the importance of digital marketing.

Terms used to describe the type of marketing we are talking about in this book have evolved in usage over time, with digital marketing currently being the most popular and on an upward trend. When I first started teaching, I taught in an e-commerce program, which emphasized selling products over the Internet. As we know, digital marketing is so

---

[3]ExactTarget. 2014. "2014 State of Marketing," *White Paper.* https://brandcdn .exacttarget.com/sites/exacttarget/files/2014stateofmarketing.pdf, (accessed January 20, 2020).

much more than selling products; it has come to encompass engagement with our customers across many types of electronic channels. With the use of Google Trends, a wonderful tool for competitive and other types of research we will discuss later in this book, we can see that the term digital marketing has experienced rapid growth and has outpaced the use of other terms to describe what we do as marketers in the modern age.

Speaking of terminology, digital marketing, as a practice, has its basis in direct marketing, which required a customer database to track and measure customer response. This marketing database later became crucial in the development of the concept of interactive marketing. Interactive marketing was a term that originated in the mid-1990s to capture and describe the fact that marketing was now a two-way conversation[4] and not just the one-way communication of the mass media world. Interactive marketing also required the use of a database that was developed by direct marketers, most importantly to address the individual customer in a relevant fashion. Along the way, Internet marketing came to mean using the Internet to facilitate the marketing process (see Figure 1.2).

The goal of interactive marketing as originally theorized by Dr. John Deighton was that marketing would become a "conversation." What Deighton and others did not foresee was the rapid expansion of the marketing conversation and the shift in control of the process from the marketer to the customer.[5] In fact, digital marketing can be defined as using any digital technology to facilitate the marketing process, with the end goal of facilitating customer interaction and engagement.[6,7]

Taking all these trends into account, Figure 1.2 shows how the term digital marketing has evolved from a process of response measurement to conversation to engagement. Engagement will be discussed in a later chapter,

---

[4]J.A. Deighton. November–December, 1996. "The Future of Interactive Marketing," *Harvard Business Review* 74, no. 6, pp. 151-60.

[5]A. Deighton and L. Kornfeld. Winter, 2009. "Interactivity's Unanticipated Consequences for Markets and Marketing," *Journal of Interactive Marketing* 23, no. 1, pp. 2-12.

[6]Gartner. 2014. "It Glossary," *Gartner.* https://blogs.gartner.com/it-glossary/digital-marketing-2/, (accessed October 13, 2019).

[7]Technopedia. 2014. "Digital Marketing." https://www.techopedia.com/definition/27110/digital-marketing, (accessed October 13, 2019).

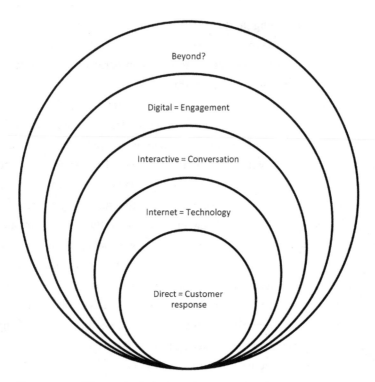

Figure 1.2 The evolution of marketing terminology from direct communication to engagement

but in short it means that customers are involved with the brand and creating and developing their own content around the brand. What will happen beyond engagement and how it will be named is anyone's guess. However, if I had to guess, I would predict a continued trend toward less control by the marketer and more control by the customer, aided and abetted by marketing technology that will be enabled to make choices for the marketer.

Digital marketing includes the ability to interactively communicate with customers through electronic channels, such as the web, e-mail, smart devices such as phones and tablets, and mobile applications. The four most recognized techniques of digital marketing are social, mobile, analytics, and e-commerce.[8]

---

[8]Gartner. 2014. "Key Findings from U.S. Digital Marketing Spending Survey, 2013," *Gartner for Marketing.* http://www.gartner.com/technology/research/digital-marketing/digital-marketing-spend-report.jsp, (accessed October 13, 2019).

These digital technologies that form digital marketing can include Internet tools such as search engine marketing and social media, customer databases, and the like. Even print processes, which now rely on digital technology, can be included broadly in this definition. As noted above, digital marketing also includes measurement and the process of customer engagement. An interesting question is, "Is all marketing digital marketing now?" Certainly, digital marketing is getting the attention of CMOs, although most of them do not think their teams are digitally ready or have the necessary skills.

For our purposes, it is useful to take a step back and realize that there have been several underlying trends that have made the development of digital marketing management a proper occupation of the executive suite. Without the convergence of these trends, shown in Figure 1.3, we would likely be looking at marketing as a different type of occupation and perhaps less relevant to the executive suite. These trends are the revolution in technology, the revolution in marketing thought, and the revolutions in communication and distribution channels.

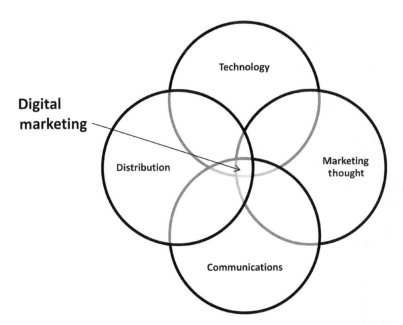

Figure 1.3 Revolutionary trends contributing to digital marketing

The Revolution in Technology

Several technologies together have facilitated the rise of digital marketing. Technologies that will be addressed here are the Internet, browsers, widespread computing, and database technology. First, the commercialization of the Internet made the technology widely available to most consumers. The Internet was developed for government use in the early 1970s by the Defense Advanced Research Projects Agency (DARPA) and used primarily for the transfer of large data files and the facilitation of communication among scientific researchers. In those days, most individuals did not have access to this vast network of information. It is useful to think of the Internet as exactly what the name implies, a network which is interconnected through technology. According to network theory, many relationships can be visualized by their relationship as nodes on a network. These nodes are represented usually as circles and the interrelationships between the circles as lines.

Almost anything can be represented by the nodes on a network. Much of social network theory represents individuals on the network as nodes and the lines represent the connections between individuals. In telecommunications theory, the nodes represent areas on the network where information is processed before moving on to another "node." Nodes tell us how our cell phones get information from one point to another as well as how information is communicated from one person to another. In Figure 1.4, Sarah is "centric" in that she knows everyone but not everyone in the network knows each other. The dark lines represent strong "ties" or relationships and the lighter lines represent weaker relationships.

Networking theory is a powerful tool for the representation of information and how it travels. Networking theory also helps to explain the phenomenal growth of the Internet as a marketing tool. The browser is a way of navigating the nodes of the Internet and is another technological innovation that spurred the growth of digital marketing. When the IT people at the university where I was teaching in 1995 installed one of the first browsers on my computer, I said to myself, "This changes everything." Because I am a business professor, what I meant when I said that everything would change was that "commerce" would change. And everything did change and is changing, more rapidly every day. What I

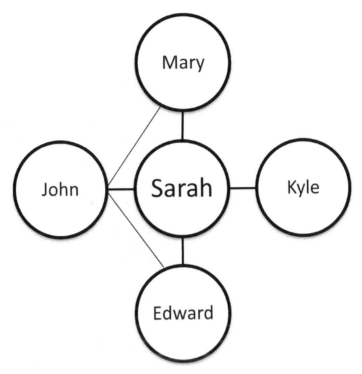

Figure 1.4 One way of representing network relations, nodes, and ties

recognized when the browser was put on top of a vast network connecting businesses and individuals was that all of a sudden it became easier to navigate the Internet. In fact, Internet technology was adopted more quickly than any previous technology, in part because of the effects of networks and how they facilitate growth and information sharing. It has taken less than 20 years for the Internet to reach 40 percent of the world's population, perhaps the most rapid growth of any technology except the mobile phone, which is also related to Internet usage. Currently, nearly 60 percent of the world's population has access to and uses the Internet for various applications. Penetration rates range from almost 90 percent in North America to nearly 40 percent in Africa. [9]

---

[9]Internet World Stats. 2019. "Internet Growth Statistics." https://www.internetworldstats.com/emarketing.htm, (accessed January 7, 2020).

Browser technology, software programs that allow the user to navigate the web, also facilitated the growth of the Internet. The first browser was called Mosaic and was developed by programmers at the University of Illinois. Other browsers rapidly followed, with the most popular today being Microsoft's Bing, Google Chrome (largest market share), and Mozilla Firefox. Of these three, only Mozilla remains as a not-for-profit company. The other firms recognized the vast commercial potential of the Internet.

In the early days of web browsers, the Internet was the domain of the young, with the typical user being the 20-something male who spent the vast majority of his time "surfing" the net. Interfaces were simple. Online chat forums are a good example of a simpler form of communication. Forums and discussion boards are a way for individuals interested in a particular topic to interact on the Internet and keep a record of their discussions. This type of interface is used to this day, but other means of communicating on the Internet have become more prevalent. The proliferation of devices with which to access the Internet also facilitated its growth. The availability of desktop and laptop computers and now mobile devices, thin clients, and notebooks means that the Internet is everywhere and literally at everyone's fingertips. Of course, the Internet would be nothing without the data behind it. Database technology is used to capture Internet transactions, place advertisements, and analyze browsing history, all leading to a more satisfactory web experience targeted to the needs of the individual customer.

The growth of the Internet would not have been possible without data processing and analysis. Just look at what happened in the bookselling industry. Amazon.com was developed as an online firm and had the ability, through a process known as "collaborative filtering" of the orders its customers made from the beginning, to make recommendations online that were based on customer preferences. Offline booksellers such as Barnes and Noble, and the now defunct Borders, struggled to differentiate themselves in the marketplace and many ultimately failed. Amazon started with an excellent database management system and did not have to play "catch up" to discover its customers' preferences and identities and now controls both the bookselling and publishing industries. Barnes and Noble developed its loyalty program to catch up and start collecting customer information. Perhaps the program has slowed the decline in sales since 2012, even if it has not reversed the downward trend. Barnes and Noble's loyalty program has aided with customer retention and club members spend more than the average customer.[10] The loyalty program data also provides valuable customer insights.

The Revolution in Marketing Thought

While technology was changing, so was the way marketers were thinking about marketing (see Figure 1.5). There has been a clear evolution from mass communication to two-way communication to interactive forms of communication. While changes were happening that allowed us to communicate directly with customers more easily, marketers were beginning to be frustrated with the traditional mass marketing approach. Mass marketing started in the 1900s and mass advertising developed with the advent of another technology, the television, in the 1950s. In mass advertising, while we might do some rough marketing segmentation (breaking customers into groups with similar characteristics) in general, the message is the same for all consumers. In direct or two-way communication, we acknowledge that customers have true differences and customize offers to

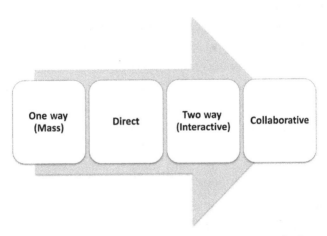

Figure 1.5 Progression of communications in marketing and advertising

---

[10]B. Unglesbee. 2019. "Can a New Owner Rewrite the Story of Barnes & Noble?" https://www.retaildive.com/news/can-a-new-owner-re-write-the-story-of-barnes-noble/557310/, (accessed January 15, 2020).

them in such a way that demonstrates we understand that uniqueness. For example, a catalog marketer might send different versions of catalogs to different targeted segments. Direct marketing therefore formed the roots of Internet marketing because of the direct marketer's use of customer databases to create a two-way form of interaction with the customer.

In true interactive marketing, we take into account what the customer has said, remember what was said, and demonstrate in our next offer to the customer that we remember what was said. We eagerly anticipate the response from the customer so we can tailor our next communication. The definition of marketing has changed from a marketplace based on a one-time exchange to a conversation that is expected to be ongoing and evolving. Rogers and Peppers popularized this notion of interactive marketing, calling it one-to-one marketing in their original book.[11] The two hypothesized a future which only later became technically possible, in which customer communications would be different for each customer based on their preferences. For this type of communication to occur, we needed the technological developments of the Internet, browsers, databases, and pervasive computing discussed earlier in this chapter.

Marketers were then able to respond to customers in a way that demonstrated that they had taken into account the customers' past history and expressed preferences. To do so they used marketing concepts such as personalization and customization. Personalization means that we use information about the customer such as name, address, and other preferences in our communications with the customer. Customization means that a product is actually built for that customer based on their preferences.[12] True customization is quite difficult to master. Think of a customized suit which requires measuring, crafting, and fitting to the individual. Mass customization, on the other hand, is quite easily handled by the technology used to facilitate the Internet. Mass customization allows the customer to select from certain preprogrammed or preset options to develop a product suited to their needs. An example of mass customization

---

[11]D. Peppers and M. Rogers. 1993. *The One to One Future* (New York, NY: Doubleday).
[12]D.L. Zahay and A. Griffin. 2003. "Information Antecedents and Consequences of Personalization and Customization in Business-to-Business Service Markets." *Journal of Database Marketing* 10, no. 3, pp. 255-271-326.

would be Nike.com, which allows the customer to create a shoe based on certain parameters, which is unique to them. Another example is modelmyoutfit.com, which allows the retail customer to see what clothes would look like on their body type.

Both personalization and customization are firm capabilities that are related to the development of the database within the corporation. The database allows the firm to develop the understanding of the customer to engage in these activities. This view of the customer is often called the 360-degree view. In other words, the firm knows about the customer, the name, the transactions history, and other supplemental or enhanced data. This data is critical to developing a marketing program that is "one to one" or targeted for the individual customer. Data means that the focus shifts from the process of marketing management from the firms' point of view to a "customer-centric" focus. A marketing program that is essentially customer-centric is focused on the needs, wants, and desires of the customer and not those of the company. This customer centricity leads to customer engagement and interaction of digital marketing, making the next step of marketing communications collaboration.

Similarly, whereas marketing efforts earlier sought to attract, acquire, and retain customers, we now seek a fourth objective—to engage customers once we have them (see Figure 1.6). We will speak more about engagement later in the book, but for our purposes now, engagement means creating customer relationships where there is a true give and take and where the customer is a partner and participant in marketing and product efforts. An example would be the difference between the old-style airline loyalty programs where users collected points and the innovative programs such as those at KLM (Royal Dutch Airlines), which uses social media engagement for everything from customer information dissemination to the decision to open new markets.[13]

As we can see, at the same time that technology was developing that enabled the collection of data about the customer and its rapid communication over the Internet, marketing thought was developing to the point

---

[13] Van der zee interviewed by Kane. 2014. "Communication with Customers through Social Media Instead of by Phone is Becoming Standard at Global Airline KLM." *MIT Sloan Management Review.*

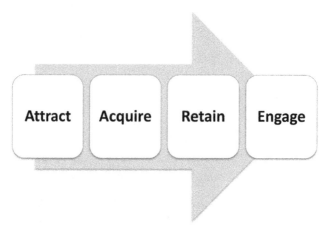

Figure 1.6 Updated customer relationship management objectives

where marketers wanted to communicate with the customer in ways that went beyond mass communications and even direct communications.

The Revolution in Communications/Distribution

It is unlikely that the evolution of digital marketing would have been possible without the development of communications and distribution channels. Technology meant that digital communications were increasingly possible, creating new methods of communication with the customer. Evolving from traditional forms of direct communication with the customer (sales, phone, fax, direct mail), e-mail was the first digital channel to emerge in the 1990s. This channel allowed marketers to communicate with the customer directly but also to more quickly respond to information gained from the customer. E-mail marketing tools also provided easy access to data about response rates and the effectiveness of varying marketing offers.

Since that time, there has been a proliferation of digital channels of communication, including social networks, text messages, RSS feeds, and so on. Communications have proliferated to the point where we can communicate with the customer at every point in the customer lifecycle and decision-making process in the manner in which the customer wishes to be communicated, which is true one-to-one marketing. In this time

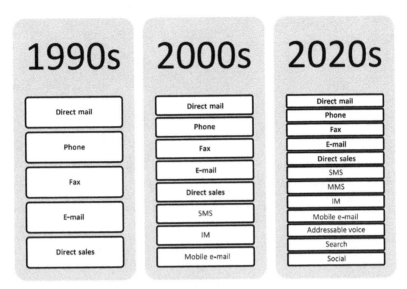

Figure 1.7 The evolution of direct media

period, a media evolution, or more accurately a media revolution, has occurred where the types of media available to the marketer have exploded. Figure 1.7 shows how much the world of direct marketing communications has changed in just over a generation, with implied challenges for marketers. From a few simple channels, we now have more ways to reach the customer than ever before, including search and social media, which can in some sense be seen as direct communication. Indirect media has evolved in an even more fragmented fashion, from simple TV, radio, print, and display advertising in the 1990s to a list that includes the following fragmented media channels:

- TV
- Radio
- Print
- Display advertising, including behavioral
- Websites
- Search, paid, and organic
- Online display
- Landing pages/Microsites
- Online video/Picture sites

- Affiliate marketing
- Webinars
- Blogs
- RSS
- Podcasts
- Wikis
- Social networks
- Mobile web/Apps
- Social media ads
- Virtual worlds
- Widgets
- QR codes/Alternatives

Another key development that facilitated Internet commerce and the rise of digital marketing management was the rise of distribution networks in the form of Federal Express, UPS, and other improvements in delivery service and technology. These networks meant that orders could be delivered quickly enough and door-to-door in such a manner that customers find ordering on the Internet an attractive alternative to brick-and-mortar shopping experiences. Without these changes, Internet shopping experiences would be considerably less appealing.

All these changes and forces resulting in the rise of digital marketing have created a situation where customer acquisition and relationship management and development are a continuous process, and one not always in the control of the marketing manager. Along each step of the way as we work to manage the marketing process, we must develop clear actions for every marketing step. As Figure 1.8 shows, objectives can be categorized as conducting research, raising awareness, branding, generating leads, acquiring customers, customer management and communication, up-selling and cross-selling, retention and loyalty, and, finally, the identification of customers who can be brand advocates. Technology plays a role each step of the way but is not the main focus of the company. As we shall see in Chapter 2, to develop an effective digital marketing strategy, the firm must first consider how it creates and delivers value.

Figure 1.8 Customer acquisition and relationship management: A continuous process

What to Do Next after Chapter 1

1. Select a major customer relationship management objective(s): attract, acquire, retain, and engage for your firm or another (Figure 1.6).
2. Develop a list of detailed objectives for that objective and for the relationship management process (Figure 1.8).
3. Define how about defining website objectives and how they might align with stated marketing objectives.

Discussion Questions

Discussion 1.1: Discuss the role the Internet plays in the lives of consumers and businesses. Has it changed the way businesses operate in any significant fashion? Can you give examples of the impact of the Internet in either B2C or B2B markets? Give an example of a company that has significantly changed its business practices because of the Internet.

Discussion 1.2: What do you think the future is for customized products? Think of an example of a product that could reasonably be customized and explain why the target customer would find value in the customization. Find an example of product customization online and discuss whether or not you think it will be successful.

Discussion 1.3: Are there other types of customer relationship management objectives that should be added to Figure 1.8? How relevant is customer relationship management (CRM) if the customer is increasingly in charge of the marketing "conversation"?

Discussion 1.4: How do you think digital marketing will evolve? Will there be more types of media in the future and what will be the goals of managing these types of media?

Glossary

Customization: Making each product uniquely for every customer.

Digital marketing: Using any digital technology to facilitate the marketing process, with the end goal of facilitating customer interaction and engagement.

Interactive marketing: Remembering what the customer tells us so marketing is a conversation.

Internet marketing: Using the Internet to facilitate the marketing process.

Mass customization: Using a predefined set of product features to allow customers to develop their own product.

CHAPTER 2

Creating the Strategic Digital Marketing Objective

With this background behind us, it is perhaps best to start thinking about the process of digital marketing management from the managerial point of view by beginning with some traditional ideas of strategic thought. In fact, it is these strategic ideas which should form the foundation of any credible search engine marketing program, and indeed, any integrated marketing communications campaign. The basic ideas of strategic thought are those of core competencies, creating value, and positioning.

The notion of core competencies comes from the resource-based view of the firm, which states that the resources a firm has form the basis of its inimitable advantage. These theories were developed by Edith Penrose,[1] Jay Barney,[2] and others. The notion of inimitable resources as a firm's core competencies, upon which firm strategy should be based, is linked to the learning organization. The learning organization theory suggests that the only true resource that a firm possesses that cannot be implemented is the ability to learn (Figure 2.1).[3]

It is precisely this notion of core competencies and the learning organization which is the first place to start in developing a search engine marketing approach within the organization. The two processes are closely related. We need to understand how we are being looked for in searches

---

[1]E. Penrose. 1959. *The Theory of the Growth of the Firm* (New York, NY: John Wiley & Sons).

[2]J. Barney. 1980. "Firm Resources and Sustained Competitive Advantage," *Journal of Management* 17, no. 1, pp. 99-120.

[3]G.S. Day. 1994. "Continuous Learning about Markets," *California Management Review*, Summer, pp. 9-31.

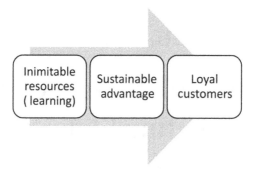

Figure 2.1 The role of learning in creating competitive advantage

and we need to convey our uniqueness to the customer so they can find us through the search process. Before we can discuss how search and strategy are more closely related, we need to introduce another basic strategic framework, the value chain.

In my consulting practice, I often come across clients who think they need a new website or brochure or want help with search engine marketing but have no idea how they are thought about in the marketplace by the customer. In addition, the search engine marketing process itself can become a way for companies to learn about the marketplace and customers. Search rankings themselves are becoming a source of competitive advantage as the firm learns from the process. Therefore, the first step in any digital marketing campaign should be to ask the questions: What is my firm all about? What makes us unique? (See Figure 2.2.)

The concept of core competency is then related to the value chain as popularized by Michael Porter,[4] with the idea that what makes the firm unique is conveyed along the value chain as the firm produces its product or service. The internal systems of the firm, such as supply chain management and operations planning, help develop the firm's value. These ideas of what makes the firm unique and the exploration of how it delivers value can then be directly tied to the firm's positioning statement. Companies that distinguish themselves on service, such as Nordstrom in the retailing space, compete on the right side of the value chain. Companies that

---

[4]M. Porter. 1985. *Competitive Advantage: Creating and Sustaining Superior Performance* (New York, NY: The Free Press), pp. 33-52.

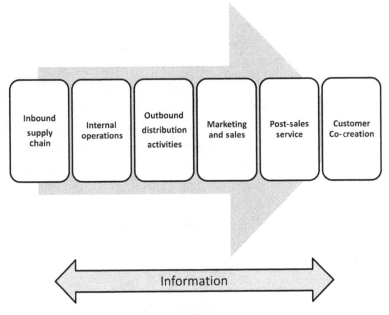

Figure 2.2 Activities leading to the creation of value for and by customers

Source: Adapted from Michael Porter.

compete upon operational efficiencies that allow them to pass along cost savings to their customers, like Wal-Mart, compete on the left side of the value chain. Along the value chain, information is disseminated and used to create value. An example of information passed along the chain to create value might be simple order processing systems. These systems help us understand who the customer is and then to deliver information to the customer along the chain. The information helps us to serve the customer and then further creates value by contributing to a complete picture of the customer that can be used to target more effectively in marketing and in selling to the customer. The customer increasingly plays a role in the process of co-creation of value in the value chain. The processes of customer relationship management, supply chain management, and product development and management add value in different ways to the firm's customers.[5] These principles are the same whether we are talking about an

---

[5]D.L. Zahay and R. Handfield. 2004. "The Role of Learning in Adoption of B2B Technologies," *Industrial Marketing Management* 33, pp. 627-41.

online or offline marketer, or, as is most often the case now, a multichannel marketer.[6]

Finally, the firm interfaces with its environment in another way. As Figure 2.3 shows, firms take in information from suppliers/partners, competitors, customers, and employees and then use that information to learn and continue to create value. Digital marketing technologies help to create that value. Each time a search or e-mail marketing campaign is executed and analyzed, the firm learns more about itself and its customers to create the next customer interaction. This is an iterative process that is facilitated by digital marketing technology. With the emphasis on one-to-one marketing and highly personalized communications, one could argue that traditional positioning, while still useful in helping to

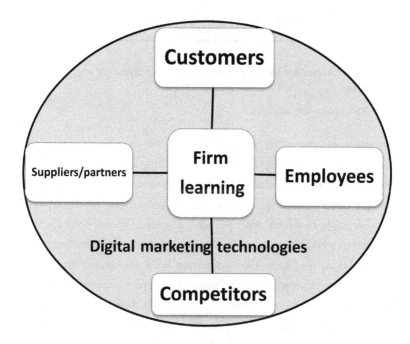

Figure 2.3 Digital marketing technologies enhance firm sensing capabilities

[6]Bange, Saara, Johanna Moisander, Rita Järventie-Thesleff, 2019. "Brand co-creation in multichannel media environments: a narrative approach", *Journal of Media Business Studies*, DOI: 10.1080/16522354.2019.1596722.

create a general messaging strategy, is somewhat irrelevant as each customer will expect messaging that demonstrates a particular product's or service's value to them as an individual. However, positioning is still a useful approach today in terms of helping understand and define uniqueness and strengths.

For today's marketer, a useful tool in developing positioning strategies can be Google Trends. This tool is important because it allows an insight into the world of the Internet on a real-time basis. Using this tool, we can type in key terms and see what is happening now and also how terms have evolved from the past. For example, when I started teaching in this area, the term e-commerce marketing represented what I did, and I taught in an e-commerce marketing program. Later, I moved to a university where I created an interactive marketing program and then I spearheaded the development of a digital marketing minor for undergraduates and a digital marketing master's degree at another university. In the process, I wrote a textbook on Internet marketing. Which term is correct for what we are discussing here?

Google Trends helped me to understand that the way people think about what I have been teaching and researching has changed over the years. I suggested the use of digital marketing for a minor in the Marketing Department where I teach now and for this book. I arrived at this determination through research. First, I wanted to see how users look at these terms, so I consulted Google Trends for search. The search indicated that the product category as defined by relevant terminology has evolved from e-commerce, which is a rather narrow term emphasizing the direct sales of products over the Internet, to interactive marketing, which focused on the conversational nature of marketing, to digital marketing, which acknowledges the increasing role played by various forms of technology in marketing and the need to foster customer engagement.

Google Trends for search indicated that interactive and Internet marketing as terms which people search for peaked in about 2004–5, e-commerce marketing in 2001, and that digital marketing is on the upswing. Therefore, if the university were to try to market the program as an e-commerce marketing program, the term would not only be narrow and not as encompassing as either interactive or digital marketing, the term would also not have as high a traffic volume as terms that are trending upward. Google Trends also gives an idea of the volume of searches, whether the term is trending upward or downward, the areas of the globe where people search for particular terms, and terms that are trending upward.

This is our first, simple case where digital marketing technology is important to managerial decisions. The recommendation here is to not make any strategic decisions in terms of our positioning statement without first consulting the world of search for one way of seeing how consumers view the world—a digital marketing technique. Although insights into our customer might once have been the exclusive province of marketing research, we now can gain insights by analyzing search trends and social media interactions, which can often be less expensive than traditional market research. Remember that value creation is still the core of business. However, technology has facilitated value creation over the value chain and also should be used to discover how best to position our product. Increasingly, value is created through networks of relationships, whether it be suppliers or customers. For example, Platform companies such as Facebook and Airbnb own few physical assets and rely on networks of relationships to deliver value.

Traditional ways of understanding the target market, such as market research surveys and focus groups, continue to be valuable ways of looking at the market. In the digital age, we can start by looking online, through searches, at what is being said about the product or service in social media, the major platforms, specialty platforms, and blog posts. The understanding of the target market can also involve digital marketing techniques such as analyzing internal and external databases and web logs to see how individuals are interacting with our website.

Using these insights and others, we can decide how our firm is unique and how it can add value to its customers. The next step in the process is usually to develop a positioning statement which we can then use to communicate our firm's value internally. For this statement, we must know (1) the target market, (2) the selection set from which the customers make their decision (product category), and (3) the firms' unique contribution to the marketplace (core competencies and value created). The format of a positioning statement can be as follows: "To the (target market), *our product* is the (product category) that (firm's uniqueness)."

There are other approaches to strategy formation, but this approach will also tie in with the search engine marketing process quite nicely in the next chapter. It is from this positioning statement that the firm communicates with its ad agency and within the company. The outside world sees the firm positioning statement in the form of a tag line such as "Like a good neighbor, State Farm is there." Or for SNICKERS˚ the most enduring tag line is "You're Not You When You're Hungry" and for Target it is "Expect More. Pay Less." The positioning statement would be more formal, such as "To those needing a mid-afternoon pick-me-up, Snickers is the snack food that satisfies hunger most quickly." Remember that we are always trying to understand how the customer views our product or service. Any combination of chocolate, nougat, caramel, and 250 to 300 calories will temporarily, at least, satisfy hunger. Snickers wants us to think of their product first when we are hungry, and this approach is the source of their advertising messaging campaign.

So the first step in the process for applying strategic principles to digital marketing is to understand that the firm itself is really an entity that takes in information from a variety of sources to learn about the customer and how best to operate in a particular competitive environment. This information needs to be constantly analyzed and updated, and digital marketing technologies provide a good source of information that can be readily analyzed and used for a competitive advantage. Therefore, digital marketing information and its processing and analysis should be central to the development of firm positioning strategy. Some examples are simple. The job search site "Indeed.com" positions itself as collecting all the information on open jobs that a job seeker might wish to have in one place, and it uses information along the value chain to create its product and communicate that value to its customers, who are both job seekers and job posters. Most examples are more complex, so understanding how information is used to create value and developing a strong positioning based on the strengths and uniqueness of the firm can help lay a firm foundation for the digital marketing efforts that we will discuss throughout the rest of this book and especially for website design, our next topic.

What to Do Next after Chapter 2

1. Develop a list of what makes your or another company unique.
2. Write down how this firm delivers value on the value chain and/or through digital platforms.
3. Put it all together: Develop a positioning statement that reflects the product categories and uniqueness and the firm's benefit to the customer.

Discussion Questions

Discussion 2.1: Discuss the value chain elements for a specific industry or company of your choosing. How does the company compete? What value-added processes are used? In terms of engagement, how does the customer help create value?

Discussion 2.2: Some firms choose to generate revenue by selling or licensing their proprietary software. Others choose an open systems approach and distribute it free of charge. What do you think drives the decision and which, if any, business approach is superior?

Glossary

Co-creation: How both the customer and the firm create value in the marketplace.

Positioning: What makes a business unique in the mind of the customer.

Positioning statement: A specific format that communicates the product, product category and uniqueness to internal stakeholders and the firm's advertising agency.

Value chain: Activities which lead to the creation of customer value.

CHAPTER 3

Web and Mobile Design

The Website: A Key Element of the Digital Marketing Delivery Mix

Effective web and mobile design is the place to begin in digital marketing. From our basic web and mobile platforms we develop strategies for other delivery platforms, which include search, social, and e-mail marketing. The platforms drive traffic to web and mobile sites for the redemption of offers, order processing and the development of customer relationships.

Therefore, how the web page is designed is critical in terms of a website being found on the Internet. In spite of the move to mobile and social marketing, the web or mobile site is still often the destination of our marketing campaigns and must be "found" online. Social media "icons" can be put on a website to refer customers to social media outlets, and it can be used to create website traffic. E-mails can also be used as part of an integrated program to drive traffic to the site and continue ongoing interactions with customers.

Once customers are on the site, it is important to make it easy for users to navigate the site and find out what they want. Much has changed since the early days of the Internet in terms of website design, but the basic principles are the same. First and foremost, determine the objectives for the website. Websites fall into two basic categories: informational and transactional. Informational websites are those that provide information but not opportunities for purchasing a product or service. Transactional websites can be for e-commerce or, in the case of a not-for-profit organization, for donations. Don't leave the decision about website objectives just to technical people. Marketers must be involved in and drive the process, always keeping the customer in mind.

Overall, we want a website that is engaging and has what is known as "stickiness" so customers will return to the site time and again. We also want, as Steve Jobs has said, something that "works" and helps the user do what they need to do. The details of web design have become more complicated as the Internet has evolved. However, the process of developing a website has remained fairly stable. One big change is that many companies now adopt a "mobile-first" strategy and develop their mobile website first so that any speed in loading issues can be resolved quickly. Since so many searches and purchases now occur on mobile devices, it does make sense to consider how the user will interface with the mobile site sooner rather than later. In this chapter, we will refer to both web and mobile site development as occurring at the same time to achieve the same marketing objectives and goals.

As Figure 3.1 illustrates, the web as a marketing tool has grown as information connection capabilities and social connections have improved. The initial era of the Internet involved getting basic information to the customer through websites and database linkage. As the web evolved, keyword search techniques and social media became more prevalent. First, we had Web 1.0,

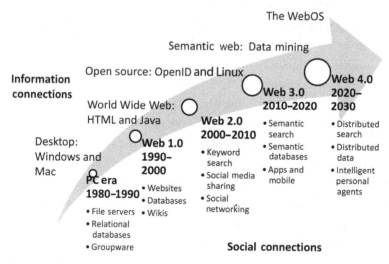

Figure 3.1 The evolution of web technology

Source: Adapted from Radar Networks and Nova Spivak: www.radarnetworks.com by Dr. Debra Zahay.

which I like to fondly call "brochureware." Brochureware was just a way of putting information on websites. With Web 2.0, marketers became more sophisticated and wanted to provide not only information but also take advantage of the interactivity of the web. This advancement required customer databases and collection of customer information to provide personalized responses and recommendations.

Now, in the world of Web 3.0, we see more sophisticated "semantic" or "contextual" search terms and the rise of mobile websites and applications. (All websites must now be designed with mobile devices in mind). As we enter Web 4.0, we will see an increasing use of marketing automation and machine learning in web applications, particularly in the form of intelligent personal agents and increasingly sophisticated search algorithms. However, a solid web and mobile development process, coupled with company strategy, will help no matter what happens in the next phase of the Web.

Customer Lifecycle Management

It is tempting to leap into the website design phase without taking a step back to figure out what our objectives are for both our firm and our website. We might also consider the customer lifecycle as a way to develop website objectives. Digital marketing management often uses the principle of the customer lifecycle to organize campaigns and programs. It is often useful when analyzing how we wish to interact with a particular customer or prospect (future customer) to consider what is known as the customer lifecycle. This form of the customer lifecycle was developed by Charlotte Mason at the University of Georgia for teaching customer relationship management (CRM) classes and is shown in Figure 3.2. There are other forms of the customer lifecycle from other business sources, but this one is comprehensive and suits the purposes of our text.

CRM relies heavily on understanding that businesses have shifted from a product-centric to a customer-centric focus and the lifecycle is used to describe these stages. These stages are based on the basic stages of the development of interpersonal relationships. The basic idea is that customers are seen as being in five major groups or stages.

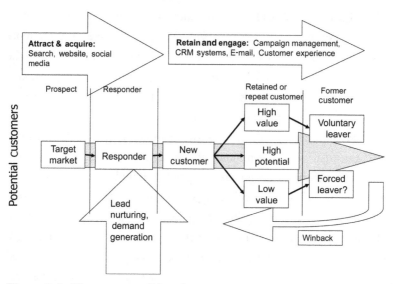

Figure 3.2 The customer lifecycle

Source: Dr. Charlotte Mason, University of Georgia, adapted with permission from Racom Communications.

Figure 3.2 shows the major stages of the customer lifecycle and is organized around Figure 1.6's "Updated Customer Relationship Management Objectives" and the five main types of customers[1]:

- Prospects
- Responders
- New customers
- Retained or repeat customers
- Former customers

The customer lifecycle starts before the customer becomes a customer (**prospect**). Likely prospects for a vacation package might be those who have traveled previously. Prospects for tablet computers may be defined by a combination of demographics (such as income exceeding $45,000

---

[1]Thanks to Charlotte Mason and Rich Hagle from Racom Communications for the reproduction of this graphic from the manuscript by L. Spiller, D. Zahay and K. Ruf, eds. *Contemporary Database Marketing and Analytics.*

and college-educated), known interests (such as photography), or product ownership (such as personal computer).

As the company reaches out to the prospect through various forms of marketing such as direct mail and e-mail, salesperson contact, the company website, and social media, any customer who asks to receive more information or wishes to engage more with the firm is called a responder. **Responders** may ask for more information online, call an 800 number, or purchase, that is, become new customers. Examples include a couple who calls a toll-free number to request information on life insurance, a person who registers at a website and asks for more information on tablet computers, or an individual who sends in the reply card requesting additional information from a direct mailing about vacation packages.

Firms usually treat new customers in a special way to show that they are welcome and often encourage them to purchase again soon to cement the customer relationship. **Retained or repeat customers** are those who purchase regularly, although they will purchase differently and have different "customer lifetime value." Those who spend a lot with us now are "high value." Typically, a small proportion of customers account for the majority of profits and these are high-value customers that the business wants to retain.

Customers with the potential to purchase from us are called "high potential," and those who do not purchase regularly and/or do not make large purchases may be considered "low value." This group of low-value customers is often unprofitable for the firm as it costs more to service them than they yield in revenues. For these customers, the goal is to convert them to profitable customers or perhaps encourage them to take their business elsewhere. In between are customers of varying profitability. Of particular interest are those that can be identified as high-potential customers. These customers are not yet in the high-value category, but appear to have the potential to be in that group if the firm is able to develop the customer relationship.

Eventually and inevitably the relationship changes and customers may drop off the lifecycle and become **former customers** (often called "churned customers"). Some customers voluntarily attrite (leave) by taking their business elsewhere. High levels of voluntary leaving or attrition (often called churn) are prevalent in long-distance and wireless phone service, Internet access, and some financial services, as customers are lured away by enticing offers from competitors. In other instances, customers may leave or attrite because they no longer need the product or service. A family may outgrow the need for children's products, or a retired couple may move to an apartment and no longer need a lawn service. In many instances it is difficult to determine when a customer becomes a former customer. Consider the regular catalog customer who doesn't make a purchase for several years or the credit card customer who stops using the card, but doesn't close the account. Are they still customers—or former customers? Finally, some customers are forced to churn if they fail to make payments.

If the relationship is seen as a potentially valuable relationship, then we can start the "winback" process to make offers and extend information that might be valuable to that customer. Also important today is the "lead nurturing" process, whereby we track customer interactions prior to purchase to try to develop the relationship so that the lead or prospect becomes a customer. We might track for a business-to-business customer whether a customer had downloaded a white paper, attended a webinar, browsed our online catalog and, according to those actions, suggest other information or perhaps send the lead to a salesperson for an in-person interaction in an attempt to win a new customer. Digital technology helps to facilitate this lead sharing process.

All along the customer lifecycle, digital marketing technology helps to facilitate the customer relationship. In the acquisition phase, many forms of digital technology are used to interface with the prospect. For example, as the customer searches for a product we might optimize our website to be found by search engines, place advertising on the site to draw the customer to the site, or engage in targeted e-mail marketing, with permission. Once the customer has been acquired, digital technologies such as e-mail communications or personalized direct mail communications are used to nurture that customer relationship to retain and engage. Also, along the way, customer feedback is important. Lead nurturing or demand generation is an important aspect of the customer lifecycle. Firms specialize in the development of systems to help score and classify leads and help nurture the customer relationship. For the purposes of website design, we may need to select lifecycle objectives for our design process.

Firm Objectives First, Website Objectives Next

It may seem that we have taken a long road to get to the discussion of what should be in the firm's website. As discussed in the strategy chapter, the firm positioning must be soundly developed first. Only then can we begin the process of website design. From a company perspective, websites, whether for a desktop or mobile device, must further the company objectives. If our positioning is highly differentiated and emphasizes customer service, our website must convey that message and reinforce the site's basic positioning. We must also make sure to reinforce this message across all delivery channels and devices, using the company website as a point of reference.

We use the term "responsive" web design to indicate that the website can be accessed and used easily across all types of devices, whether it be a tablet, desktop, or mobile phone. This type of responsive design is important because multichannel shoppers typically purchase more than single channel shoppers. The goal is to create a seamless, cross-channel, and cross-device experience.

Cross-device marketing isn't just about responsive web design; all aspects of the company's digital marketing strategy often come into play. For example, people search differently on mobile devices than desktops. Mobile devices tend to be more social so when customers search for "hood" on a mobile device, they mean their neighborhood. When they search for "hood" on a desktop device, they often mean "hoodie" or an article of clothing. This difference has implications for web design, search, and social media marketing. Targeted mobile apps might be used for customer retention to allow access to loyalty program information at the customer's fingertips.

Cross-device planning is greatly enhanced by analytics. We marketers are often reluctant to create applications for a certain device, but today we can access data and show which devices and operating systems are driving traffic to the website. Usually data helps overcome any reluctance to develop for a particular platform.

But before we select our platforms, we must select goals and objectives for our web/mobile site. Different companies and not-for-profits will have different objectives depending on their goals and objectives. One firm might wish to increase sales revenue, another visibility and branding, and so on. One way to select objectives is to develop them according to the customer acquisition and relationship management continuum (Figure 1.8) discussed in Chapter 1.

We might be using our website to create awareness or branding or for more measurable objectives like lead generation and customer acquisition. We might also develop site objectives along the stage of the customer lifecycle. Whatever the method used, it is important to have objectives. Website objectives, as you will remember from Chapter 2, come from the company's own strategy and positioning. Objectives are usually driven by both the marketing strategy and objectives (and before that the business goals) and the target audience.

Another way to develop site objectives is to look at the websites of competitors and see how they are targeting their site and who their customers are. Free tools such as Google Analytics and other paid tools such as Alexa.com, IBM Digital Analytics, and Adobe Analytics help us see where our website traffic is coming from and help us refine our goals. Whatever method we use, we must have website goals that align with our strategic goals, first and foremost.

Targeting and Personas: Who Is Using the Site?

Once we have our goals, we must closely define our target market for the site. It's not that we are going to turn away people who are not our "ideal" customer, it is just that we are designing the site for those we wish to make the most use of our site. In the traditional marketing world, we use the concept of market segmentation extensively. We find groups of customers with similar characteristics and then market to them accordingly. We might group customers under a similar heading such as "soccer moms" or "empty nesters," using demographic and lifestyle characteristics to explain these types of behaviors. The digital world calls for understanding more complex behaviors. Therefore, we make use of the concept of the persona in developing our understanding of our marketplace. The persona is used to understand a customer's habits as well as characteristics, particularly the habits of social media usage. We use the persona to describe preferences and behaviors that might not necessarily be available through standard segmentation methods.

A market segment is a homogenous subgroup of a heterogeneous aggregate market that is selected as a target market. However, a persona is a fictionalized description of the likely customer for the product, including a rich description of behaviors and preferences. A persona, instead of focusing on customer characteristics, focuses on customer experiences. If we are marketing coffee drinks, we might describe a typical day in the life of "Java Joe" who is a 20-something professional living in a large urban area. Traditional segmentation often relies on customer demographics such as age and zip code, and might even get into some of the segment's psychological and behavioral characteristics in the aggregate. Java Joe's persona description, in contrast, might talk about how he spends his day and structures it around the experiences with coffee. In narrative form we might say, "Joe typically starts his day with a cup at home with his significant other and then grabs a cup on his way to work; mid-afternoon he takes a break at the local coffee shop and engages in conversation there while checking e-mail and texts on his phone. He has subscribed to text message and e-mail updates from his favorite coffee shop and also has the app installed on his mobile phone. Joe likes to comment on Facebook about our product and frequently interacts with the web page. Joe also writes a coffee blog which captures his daily experiences and likes to end the day with an aromatic cup of decaf."

To further highlight the difference between the persona and the segment, consider the B2B marketing world. The most basic form of market segmentation is the division between ultimate consumers and B2B markets. For example, in standard segmentation for B2B companies, there are five major data items that are used by B2B marketers to augment or enhance their internal data. These items are Standard Industrial Classification (SIC) or North American Industry Classification System (NAICS) code, company size, company revenue, number of employees, and geographic location (Chapter 9). Beyond that, the information becomes quite specific to the industry. For example, companies selling computer software to be installed internally might want to know what operating system or systems the company was using. If we were to apply the concept of personas to companies, we would use more descriptive information, such as the type of company in terms of its personality, hiring style, or atmosphere at work, things that cannot necessarily be described by standard segmentation.

Site Content and Design

Whether we are using segmentation or personas to define our target market, we then design site content appropriate for the target market. For example, Office Depot® Office Max® targets its various business segments (small business, home user, etc.) by providing them specifically designed web pages to meet their needs.[2] It is often best to decide who the target market is and what the objectives are and to develop a list of relevant content before beginning the web design process itself. Companies often focus more on the layout of the site, the font, and other design aspects and less on the actual content of the site. As we will discuss in the social media chapter, a content marketing strategy means deciding our brand story and disseminating relevant content across all channels, including the web. Therefore, our site content must be consistent with content disseminated on other channels.

In addition to content, site navigation is an important part of the actual website design process. Eyeball "tracking" studies examine how users look at websites. As we can see from Figure 3.3, most of the traffic on a website is in the upper left hand corner, known as the "golden triangle."[3] Users typically also focus on an area known as "above the fold" (from the old newspaper term) and rarely scroll down further to examine content on the bottom of the page. For mobile site design and mobile apps, the triangle becomes more of a rectangle as users tend to look at the middle of the device. There are other ways to tell how users are behaving on our specific page. We can bring the users in to testing labs or use automated tools such as "Clicktale.com" to see how users are navigating through our site with their mouse clicks. This type of website is a good surrogate for the more

---

[2]M. Roberts and D. Zahay. 2013. *Internet Marketing: Integrating Online and Offline Strategies* (Mason, OH: South–Western Cengage Learning), p. 324.

[3]L.M. Pixelrage. 2015. "Get a Heat Map for Your Website," *Hubpages*. https://hubpages.com/business/heat-map, (accessed October 13, 2019).

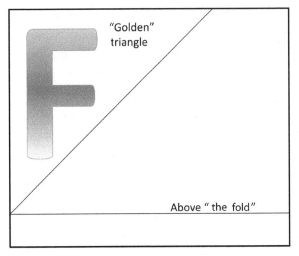

**Figure 3.3 The F pattern and the golden triangle
in website design**

expensive "eyeball" testing, where user eye movement is tracked using sensitive and expensive machines designed for that purpose.

In general, website design has evolved to a broader understanding of how human beings interface with information of any type. Humans are cognitive "misers" and seek shortcuts to understanding. That means we don't want to spend a lot of time on a site figuring out how a site works. We just want it to work. A general rule of thumb is that it should take no more than two or three clicks to get where the user needs to go or they will lose interest, usually in a few seconds. This principle is known as website "navigation" and we seek to make the navigation process easy for the consumer.

If one of our website objectives is conversion, we might also consider how the human brain processes certain information. How people respond to web and mobile sites is often deeply ingrained in our brains. Our brain is designed to filter out unnecessary information from all the information we are bombarded with every day. Therefore, we can use certain words and colors to try to trigger a response which will get our offer noticed by the customer. A good source for more information on this topic is Tim Ash's book *Landing Page Optimization*.[4] This book and other publications and websites provide insight into the behavioral aspects of website design.

---

[4]T. Ash, R. Page & M. Ginty2012. *Landing Page Optimization, Second Edition*, (Indianapolis, IN: John Wiley and Sons).

Some other important design tips include making sure that we include our important keywords for organic and paid search on our site, avoiding flash and automatically loading videos, setting up the page in columns for ease of design and use, and testing on multiple platforms. Using dark, readable fonts on a white or light background will ensure that your content is not only displayed but also easily read by the user.

Marketers often enjoy using a web content management system (CMS) so they can make changes to the site without consulting a programmer every step of the way. Cascading style sheets (CSS) can be used to ensure that the same fonts and design formats are used throughout the site. "Wireframes," paper and interactive prototypes, and site maps are tools that can help us see what the website will look like before we begin the expensive coding process.

One final note is about accessibility. For legal and practical purposes, we need to design our web and mobile sites for those who have visual, auditory, motor, or cognitive impairment. For example, a simple site map overview and large print can aid someone with a visual impairment. Closed captions and transcripts on videos can aid those with hearing disabilities. All these tools and considerations need to be included for effective website design.

Usability Testing/Launch/Measurement

Once we have determined the site objectives, we usually develop the site according to a process that includes something known as usability testing. In all cases, we want to develop the site according to the user expectations. "Usability" testing should determine that the site is easy to navigate and that users can get what they want from the site. Usability means just that—how easy it is for the user to navigate through and use our site. We can rate our site as Forester does based on value, navigation, presentation, and trust or on our own set of criteria. For example, for a transaction-based site we can include metrics about the ease and clarity of the checkout process. We would also want to analyze metrics around shopping cart abandonment.

Another often-used metric is the A/B test. A/B testing is a process whereby we test one version of the site against another. We usually test the existing version against a particular change to see what is most effective in achieving our goals. Multivariate testing involves making multiple site changes at a time and testing the results. Both of these techniques can be used for testing in other marketing channels, such as e-mail marketing, but are quite prevalent in testing website effectiveness. A fun site is guessthetest.com, which every day provides a new A/B test for analysis. You can test your skills in direct marketing and website design to see if your judgment is correct in terms of the best performing website design, e-mail, or other offers.

We can and should test the website from both a technical point of view and a marketing point of view. Not only should the website work efficiently and as expected, but it should also achieve marketing objectives. We can test in the laboratory, with our early or "beta" users, or just ask for customer feedback, or do all of the above. The important thing is to test before launch and avoid making critical mistakes. A number of metrics, such as number of clicks to make a purchase, whether the user stayed on the website for a certain time, or if they downloaded or accessed certain information, can help us determine if we are meeting our objectives.

We want to also make sure that the entire customer experience (CX), or the customer's overall interactions with the company, has been satisfactory. Customer experience management and CRM are subjects of another chapter but are relevant to web design as the website is often the first place where we have an encounter with a customer. Today's website designers weave in customer experience elements into the website by including links to social media sites for future engagement, videos, games, and other forms of customer interaction. The process of web design is ongoing. Almost immediately after we launch our site, we begin analyzing the site's performance to improve the customer's experience and the site's performance.

Future Challenges

As seen above, web and mobile design has undergone certain changes over the years as technology and the platforms for social interaction have developed and the customer experience has gone "mobile." Many marketing challenges remain in the web design world. Too many marketing channels can decrease the nimbleness of response as marketers struggle to keep current. Certainly, marketers will be continuing the cross-device and cross-platform juggling act for many years to come. Devices will continue to proliferate and be more sophisticated and marketers must meet the challenge.

Although responsive web and mobile design—design that is available and accessible to the user across all platforms—is important, many firms still struggle to meet this challenge. Typically, budgets are still "siloed," often making it difficult to free up the funds for mobile marketing or other platforms. Whatever the internal challenges, the bottom line is firms should strive to make it easy for customers to access their web and mobile sites and engage with them.

What to Do Next after Chapter 3

1. Make a list of the broad marketing objectives for your firm or another of your choosing using "attract, acquire, retain, and engage."
2. Develop a list of specific web/mobile goals according to these broad objectives. In this case be specific, that is, "Customers should come to the site to register."
3. Map your objectives and goals (Figure 1.6 and/or Figure 1.8) to the customer lifecycle (Figure 3.3). What else is needed to make these plans a reality?

Discussion Questions

Discussion 3.1: Which web or mobile sites do you think are designed particularly well and why? Pick two or three sites and analyze using the criteria in the chapter and your own experience.

Discussion 3.2: What are some of the issues marketers should consider when trying to make the conversion process on their websites as effective as possible? How can personas and purchase scenarios be helpful?

Glossary

A/B testing: Comparing one test treatment to another in web design, e-mail marketing, direct mail, or any other communications medium.

Above the fold: An old newspaper term that indicates, for effective web design, that users should not have to scroll down past the first screen of information to effectively use the website.

Customer experience: The way a customer interacts with a website or a company.

Customer lifecycle: Stages in the relationship with the customer and actions taken along those stages.

Golden triangle: An imaginary triangle on the upper left corner of a website where most site viewing occurs.

Prototypes: Nonworking website models.

Responsive web design: Designing sites so they can be used effectively no matter which desktop or mobile delivery device is used.

Site maps: Outlines of the hierarchy of the site that are useful to search engines when categorizing site material.

Stickiness: Likelihood that users will return to the site.

Wireframes: Rough sketches of what a website should look like on paper or in digital format.

PART II

Delivery

CHAPTER 4

Search Engine Marketing

This chapter is the first of three chapters that involve putting positioning strategy to work (delivery). In this chapter we will discuss both aspects of search engine marketing (SEM), paid and organic search, as well as the search marketing process and how it relates to positioning strategy and branding. At the end of this section you should have a better idea about how search relates to digital strategy.

The Search Process and Strategy

Since we have decided that the basic tenets of corporate strategy apply in the world of digital marketing, we can then apply these tenets in the world of search. There is an old adage that if you don't know where you are going, any road will get you there. The same idea can be applied in SEM. If you don't know who you are and who you are trying to target, then you won't be able to figure out how you need to present yourself on the web.

I like to say that search really is strategy. The reason I say this is that search is how people find your product. Most purchases today start with an online search, making an online search presence critically important. As stated previously, it is estimated that 93 percent of purchase decisions begin with search, so if a company doesn't know who it is or what keywords are important to customers, it can't be found online.[1]

Critical to search marketing is the concept of the keyword. In this context, a keyword is a word or phrase that users employ to search on the

[1]Dirr. 2013. "Oracle's Social Selling Expert Reveals B2B Secrets." https://blog.inside-sales.com/social-selling-2/oracles-social-selling-expert-reveals-b2b-secrets/, (accessed October 13, 2019).

Internet, hoping to get to the information they need. Sometimes users type in actual questions as keywords. The term keywords can be used loosely because keywords are increasingly phrases. As users have become more sophisticated in search, they want to target exactly what they are seeking. Google understands this trend and has changed its search engine to accommodate these longer searches. The key to finding the right keyword is to know your customers and prospects well and what their *intention* is when they search.[2] The role of customer intent in developing a search strategy is critical. Increasingly, consumers are using voice search and longer phrases to find exactly what they want. So keywords might be strings such as "cheap movie tickets near me" rather than "movie tickets." In addition to talking to our customers and using Google Trends, tools like the keywordtool.io, the Moz Keyword Explorer, and the Keyword Planner in Google Ads help us to see common search trends and understand the customer's search intention. The technology has also improved to the point where visual search is now more commonplace and must be part of a search marketing strategy.

The process of search marketing is called SEM. Essentially there are two different types of search with which marketers are concerned with (see Figure 4.1). These types of search are paid search, often called pay per click

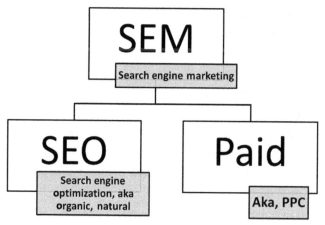

Figure 4.1 Types of search engine marketing

---

[2] I. Everdell. 2014. "SEMPO Chat on Google's Changing SERP Layout and Implications for Business." https://www.youtube.com/watch?v=YUxzpc8VRRI, (accessed March 1, 2020).

(PPC), and unpaid search. The process of paying for search involves paying for advertisements that show up on the top or the side (and sometimes the bottom) of the search engine results page (SERP). The SERP is what is shown when we type an inquiry into a search engine. It typically displays both paid and unpaid search results. This type of search marketing that uses advertising is called paid search because the advertiser pays the website hosting the advertising (Google, Yahoo!, Bing, etc.) every time someone clicks on an advertisement.

Paid Search

Paid search must be considered in terms of strategy as well. Paid search means advertisements that show up at the top and side (sometimes the bottom) of SERP. For Google search results, people tend to look vertically, which means that the sponsored ads on the right side of the page were being viewed less. While 36 percent of clicks are on the fourth position or higher, even being in the first position in paid search is not important if no one clicks on the ad or if you don't get the desired results. When setting up a paid search campaign through Google, Yahoo!, Bing, or any other vendor, keywords are critically important. Again, the appropriate keywords must match how a product or service is perceived by the customer, their search intention, and how they search for the category. Google Ads is the best known and used form of paid search, but paid search advertising can also be employed in other search engines, blogs, and increasingly on social media platforms such as Facebook.

In Google Ads, for example, we can set up how we want to be displayed based on match type, as noted in Figure 4.2. Users can search using the modifiers and punctuation below to increase their chances of a relevant search result. The type of match selected depends on the product and the campaign results. In general, a broad match will give us the most advertising display but not necessarily the most relevant results, so a modifier can help.

Phrase match is often the best choice because it will display our ad as a variation of a phrase that may be relevant to our campaign objectives. It is always good to include negative (sometimes called excluded) matches such as things for which we don't want to be found. For example, if we

Match type	Special symbol	Example keyword	Ads may show on searches that	Example searches
Exact match	[keyword]	[women's hats]	are an exact term and close variations of that exact term	women's hats
Phrase match	"keyword"	"women's hats"	are a phrase, and close variations of that phrase	buy women's hats
Broad match modifier	+keyword	+women's +hats	contain the modified term (or close variations, but not synonyms), in any order	hats for women
Broad match	none	women's hats	include misspellings, synonyms, related searches, and other relevant variations	buy ladies hats
Negative match	-keyword	-women	are searches without the term	baseball hats

Figure 4.2 *Match types for selection in Google Ads*

sell hats but not baseball hats, we can include baseball and baseball hats as negative matches.

An important aspect of paid search is the cost of the campaign. When someone clicks on an ad, the company placing the ad pays the vendor the cost, known as a "click." Paid search can be expensive, with the average cost per click (CPC) being at least between one and two dollars. Therefore, from a strategic point of view, managers are sometimes unwilling to be involved in paid search programs. The fear is that the program is a "black box" and that money will be thrown into the search marketing program and not recovered on a timely or cost-efficient basis.

The Process

The best way to manage this process is to make sure that you are using a search firm that understands the search process and to have a clear plan, or if you are doing this yourself also to have a clear plan in place. You will need to plan and make adjustments along the way based on the immediate feedback the Internet provides. A planning process can apply to both paid and organic search. A suggested process is shown in Figure 4.3. The process begins with researching appropriate keywords and their costs, building the campaign, launching and then analyzing, and reporting. Typically for paid search campaigns on Google there will be analytics such as average ad position, quality score, and CPC. The quality score is essentially the relevance of terminology on the advertiser's web page to the keywords which they are using. More specifically, quality score consists of expected click-through rate, the landing page relevance, and ad relevance, or how well the ad matches what the user is searching for at that time. For organic search programs it will be necessary to use Google analytics and/or another analytical tool to understand where your search traffic is coming from and which keywords are most effective in the campaigns.

Figure 4.3 Four main phases of search engine marketing planning

The process alone suggests that the search campaign be broken into manageable and measurable sections so as to clearly measure the results. In Google Ads these segments or sections are called ad groups. By setting up groups for different products or offers, you can measure the results of campaigns. You can also do online testing of particular campaigns and ads versus what has worked previously (known as A/B testing as discussed in Chapter 3) and conversion tracking. A conversion is anything that you want to happen as the result of your marketing efforts, or a desired action on the part of the customer. In the case of a paid search campaign, we often send those who click to a specific landing page, again for tracking purposes. These landing pages then can have a "conversion" action on them, like clicking through to another website or purchasing a product or downloading a white paper.

Figure 4.4 shows how an account can be set up in any paid search environment. This structure can apply, for example, to ads in both Facebook and Google or any other paid search format. From a managerial perspective, it is the researching and organizing of the account sublevels that is most critical. Without these levels, it is impossible to determine results and to allocate budget. There might be different campaigns for selling products like mobile access devices such as tablets versus the newer smartphone models. One campaign can be for the East Coast and another for the West Coast and have a different focus; campaigns can be set up as branded or nonbranded. Once you have established campaign themes, then you can set up different groupings known as ad groups with different keywords and ads associated with them for measurement purposes—selling Apple versus Android products, for example.

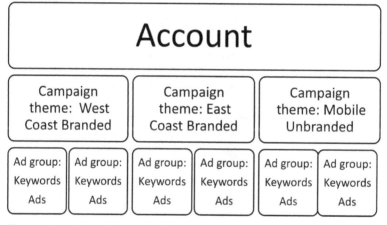

Figure 4.4 Organizing a paid search campaign

Advertisers in Ads also have the option to display on the search network or the display network, which allows them to show the ads on websites that are most relevant to those buying your product. The search network is the general network that we see when searching Google. The display network allows ads to be targeted on relevant sites such as *The Wall Street Journal* for financial products or a sports site for a weight loss product. For Facebook advertising, it is possibly to target specific demographics.

I heard of someone bidding on such a specific demographic in terms of age, sex, and location that he was able to deliver a highly targeted anniversary wish to his wife on Facebook! Google has even more targeted demographic capabilities, in acknowledgment of the importance of audience targeting. Advertisers can also target audiences that are searching for similar products.

Whatever the target market and the goal, it is most important to have a process in place for both paid and organic search, to know who the target market is and to understand the importance of each element of the campaign. For paid search, a budget is important. Search, once the alternative for those marketers who were cost-conscious, has now become big business and expensive, so keywords must be carefully chosen and budgets managed effectively.

In fact, paid search marketing is so big that the industry is predicted to reach $45 billion by 2020, and is still growing at a double-digit percent rate.[3] Google dominates the search market with an almost 70 percent share globally,[4] taking most of its growth recently from declining market shares at Yahoo!. Google's historic dominance has come from it being considered a trusted organic search source that returns the best results.

In paid search, as mentioned above, advertisers create ads and bid on the keywords, paying when a searcher clicks on the ad. The paid search process is somewhat akin to an auction, but the top-ranked ad does not always go to the highest bidder. Other factors such as quality score (expected click-through rate, landing page experience, and ad relevance) can determine how well placed the ad is on the search page and if it gets served at all. The order of the ad is referred to as the ad position, with the top ad having position 1, the next position 2, and so on. Advertisers typically try to be somewhere between positions 2 and 3 to avoid paying too much for their ad placement. Most clicks occur in the first few positions.

---

[3]eWeek. 2015. "Mobile Display Ad Market Improves Ahead of Holiday Season." https://www.eweek.com/small-business/mobile-display-ad-market-improves-ahead-of-holiday-season, (accessed October 13, 2019).

[4]Netmarketshare. 2014. "Desktop Search Engine Market Share," *Realtime Web Analytics with No Sampling.* http://www.netmarketshare.com/search-engine-market-share.aspx?qprid=4&qpcustomd=0, (accessed October 13, 2019).

Usually, on a desktop or larger tablet, users look at the top ads and do not scroll down to position 10.

A trend is the variety of choices that are now available for paid advertisement. In addition to the standard text ad, users have a chance to create ads that are targeted to shopping or are video-based. These ads can also be targeted specifically to mobile devices. An increasing number of searches are being conducted on mobile devices, so much so that Google changed its format to expand the text available to accommodate the needs of mobile users. There is more text available so that the user has more information before clicking on the ad, which is especially important in mobile advertising.

This move to mobile means that ads must be targeted, and bidding strategies must be optimized to obtain not just the first three positions, but the first one or two positions. Google now provides an Optimization Score as well as paid search recommendations to help advertisers in this competitive environment. Both of these tools can be used to make sure the campaign is performing at its best.

There is simply not enough "real estate" available on the mobile device so advertisers need to try to make sure their campaigns are the most effective. Paid search advertising has also become more competitive in general. There are other outlets for paid search, such as Instagram and other social media formats that are competing for advertising dollars. In addition, it is estimated that 50 percent or more of product searches now begin on Amazon.com.[5]

Another trend that is making search more competitive is the move to automation. Automated bidding strategies such as those employed at Google make use of machine learning and artificial intelligence to suggest the best strategy. Although some writers warn against a "set it and forget it" strategy as the best way to spend a lot of money on Google and not necessarily get a return on investment, automated strategies are a trend for the future. The Performance Planner tool is a way to try using forecasting and simulation to see how effective campaigns might be before investing a lot of money in them.

---

[5]K. Garcia. 2018. "More Product Searches Start on Amazon." https://www.emarketer.com/content/more-product-searches-start-on-amazon, (accessed January 16, 2020).

Organic Search

This careful process of planning and measurement relates to organic search as well. The unpaid type of search is known as organic or natural search and the process of getting ranked "naturally" is known as search engine optimization (SEO). This SEO process involves an understanding of what is known as a search algorithm. An algorithm helps the search engine decide which pages come closest to which queries on the Internet. The natural or organic search results show up below and to the left side of the advertisements on the SERP. Google makes changes to the search algorithm periodically. These changes are usually given a colorful name such as Penguin or Panda. One major algorithm change was called Hummingbird, which was designed to be fast and accurate. One of the latest developments is that Hummingbird has made it more difficult for smaller companies to show up in search results because of an increased emphasis on corporate branding. Increasingly you might see results from larger companies because they have a stronger brand.[6] Another change is the emphasis on "semantic" or "conversational" search. However, the basic principles of SEO remain intact.

The BERT update (Bidirectional Encoder Representations from Transformers) incorporates a greater understanding of natural language. This capability allows Google to identify nuances in search to provide the best results. The best way to work with BERT is to write better content and continue to focus on intent and the audience experience. This preference of search engines to rank sites with great content has been a trend in natural search for a long time. More recently, the algorithms have been updated to emphasize 'mobile-first indexing,' which means the mobile site is the baseline for determining search rankings.

In fact, there is a challenge today in that it is getting harder to get ranked highly in organic search results, especially for smaller companies that cannot put a lot of resources into writing engaging content. Another factor in search rankings that has increased in recent years is that of EAT (expertise, authoritativeness, and trustworthiness). These factors also tend to favor larger companies, or at least those with strong brands. That factor is one reason why this book begins with strategy and branding and

---

[6]Search Engine Land. 2014. "FAQ: All About the New Google 'Hummingbird' Algorithm," *SEO*. http://searchengineland.com/Google-hummingbird-172816, (accessed October 13, 2019).

continues to emphasize understanding who your customer is and how your company is positioned in the mind of the consumer.

While there are many factors that result in a high ranking in natural search and while the basic principles remain fairly constant, it is important to stay abreast of algorithm changes across all platforms. The basic idea behind organic search for a company is still what has been emphasized in the chapter. You must have a good idea of who the company is to choose the right keywords for web landing pages and therefore to be found by search engines when users are looking for your type of product or service. Increasingly, especially if you are logged into your Gmail account while searching, you will see results in search that are specific to you; no longer will everyone see the same results, but you will see results dependent upon your most recent searches. The content on the site is emphasized more and more frequently and it is less important to have lots of inbound links and more important to have relevant ones.

Brands are important in natural search because the search engine is trying to identify the most credible information. How organic search works is that web "crawlers," "robots," or "spiders" search the web and index content on an index server to be retrieved when a user makes a query. The results are called the SERP. Most readers are probably familiar with these pages, which look slightly different depending on the browsers. As noted above, the organic search results are usually listed above, below or to the left of the results from paid search, giving the user a complete picture of the products and services available on the web.

For organic search, a number of other factors are important in terms of rankings. Studies show that people typically do not go beyond that first page for search results so it is important to rank highly. As stated above, this high ranking is even more important on mobile sites where there is less space and fewer positions available. In addition to keywords mentioned above, other important factors are the content on the site and the authority on the site. Authority is established through inbound and outbound links to the site, suggesting that the information is relevant to a number of users. Authority is also established by the type of site. Those sites that are associated with educational institutions (.edu) often rank highly in organic search because of their domain authority. Recently, with the updates to the Google algorithm, content has increased in relevance.

Since relevant content will also improve your company's rankings on search engines, it is even more important to figure out the brand story and how to convey that story best not only through keywords but relevant content.

Content can be blog posts, white papers, news articles, social media posting, or any media that is getting the message across. But the type of content shared should not be advertising in nature. For example, if I were marketing a university, I would have information for users on how to select a university, navigate financial aid, and so on and not just talk about how great the university is. A descriptive URL with a meaningful title tag is also helpful in organic search. The title tag is an opportunity to explain your company in terms of keywords and branding and, depending on the browser, appears in the blue bar when you search and/or in the search results themselves. So the URL for the university might describe the university name, but the title tag would also include something relating to its point of difference.

Images can't be read by spiders, so it is important to tag images as well use what are known as "alt tags" or "alt text" and to have a descriptive title tag for the web page. In fact, different types of media can be quite useful in improving organic search rankings. I tried for years at a prior university to get my interactive marketing certificate program listed on the first page in organic search for certain terms, to no avail. However, once we incorporated student videos into the site from a class project, we got our desired page one ranking in a matter of weeks. Search engines, and Google in particular, reward rich media.[7]

Another factor in search engine rankings is your firm's social media usage in general. Be sure to claim your Google Business Profile and complete the profile. Other tips include Facebook page listing and making sure your online yellow and white page listings are identical. Combining rich media with social media is another way to increase your organic search rankings under the current algorithm. These organic search factors are summarized in Figure 4.5.

---

[7]A. Goldman. 2011. *Everything I Know about Marketing I Learned from Google* (New York, NY: McGraw-Hill), pp. 269-70.

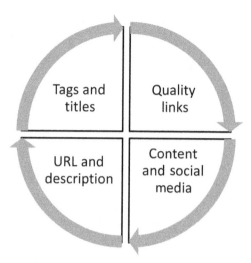

Figure 4.5 Factors for ranking in organic search

Choosing the Right Keywords

So to summarize, before you seek to implement a SEO program you need to first undertake a positioning strategy as stated in prior chapters. You need to figure out who your target customers are and how they think about your product. A common method of developing a positioning strategy is to develop the positioning statement as noted in Chapter 2. The positioning statement is used online to explain within the company the characteristics of the ideal customer or the super heavy user (SHU). This is the person to whom most mass advertising is targeted and also those who will be targeted by direct and other methods.

As stated above, keywords are important because this is how users find you online. It is a good exercise to observe those in your target market and how they search for products. A common mistake is to bid on your product name and not the need it is trying to serve. One example is the product "Monster Spray," a fanciful product to help parents allay the fears of children who are afraid of the dark. Parents can use the spray and thus calm their children's fears of monsters under the bed or in the closet.[8]

---

[8]M. Roberts and D. Zahay. 2017. *Internet Marketing: Integrating Online and Offline Strategies.* 4th ed. (Mason, OH: South-Western Cengage Learning), pp. 177-78.

Parents searching for this type of help don't search for a particular product. So bidding on "Monster Spray" might not be that effective. Instead, parents use terms such as "child afraid of the dark." Increasingly, users are searching for the answers to questions such as "What can I do if my child is afraid of the dark?" and the search engines, such as the recent Google algorithm updates, are seeking to answer these questions. This development in terms of trying to answer natural language queries and take into account the context of the search is called "semantic search."

So how can a company best align strategy/branding and search? I have previously talked in Chapter 2 about the positioning statement format. Let's assume we are marketing an Internet site for Monster Spray. The positioning exercise might look like this:

Target customer: The target may be thought of as a segment, that is, adults with small children.

Category: Product category—how you would like to be thought of by the customer, that is, tool for children afraid of the dark.

Point of difference: Your point of difference, again, in the mind of the consumer. For our site, it might be that the imaginary spray idea works effectively and gently.

Finally, a positioning statement might be: To adults with small children, Monster Spray is the parental tool for children afraid of the dark that works effectively and gently.

So how does all this relate to search? In both paid and organic search, it is important that the keywords on your web and mobile site's home page relate to the search terms that are on that page. Develop the positioning statement and then the website or landing page next. In organic search we use the term keyword density. Usually we want a keyword density on a page of 1 to 2 percent so the spiders know that the page is relevant to the topic but not disproportionally so as to indicate we are trying to "game" the search engine. The more you know and develop your brand and select relevant keywords, the more likely you will be able to be found by search engines (Figure 4.6).

We want relevant keywords or phrases, such as "afraid of the dark" to be displayed on that page. The way natural search works is the spiders or

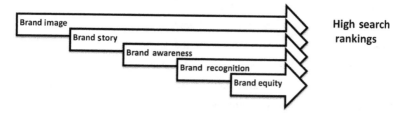

Figure 4.6 How branding aids organic search

automated programs "crawl" the web looking for keywords most relevant to the query using search algorithms. There are many elements to search algorithms and SEO experts are always trying to guess the algorithms. One thing we do know is that it is important for both SEO and PPC to have relevant keywords on the exact web page you want to come up in search results, often called a "landing page" or "microsite." Therefore, the first step in SEM is deciding who you are and what is relevant to your product or service, who your customers are, and basic company strategy. Only then can you know why they search, how they search, and what terms they use are critical to doing well in the search process. Using the process above, research keywords, put them on your website and in your paid search campaigns, measure and monitor the results, and then make changes accordingly.

Synergies between Paid and Organic Search

There is evidence that paid and organic search work together. In general, the more "real estate" you have on the page, the more people looking for your type of product will pay attention. Having both a paid and organic search campaign means that your message will be reinforced. Typically, overall interest in a company increases when they start running paid advertisements. In working with students and their clients for the Google Online Marketing challenge, we have noted that phone and other inquiries increase after a few weeks and might stop or slow down when the paid search campaign ends. I have also seen information to this effect presented at practitioner conferences. While I have not seen a good study that is able to measure the offline impact of search, there is also some academic evidence that paid and display advertising work together.

Paid and Display Ads Can Influence Each Other

An academic study by Pavel Kireyev, Koen Pauwels, and Sunil Gupta indicates that the paid search and display ad budgets can work together to create results.[9] These academics found some interesting results using data from a U.S. bank that used display advertising to obtain new checking account customers.

The display advertising generated more search volume, clicks, and conversions but the effect took about 2 weeks. The authors were also able to make some attributions regarding budgeting decision. According to these calculations, a dollar invested in display ads returns $1.24 and a dollar invested in search ads returns $1.74, which would suggest a far larger investment (36 percent increase) in search advertising in this context.

As the authors note, standard measurements such as CTR and cost per acquisition are static measures that don't take into account what may happen over time. This study suggests that managers need to step up their game in terms of metrics in order to capture these search effects accurately. The metrics are beyond those normally used in practice. Search and social media can also work together, as we will discuss in a future chapter.[10]

Branding and Search Rankings

Finally, one of the most important aspects of SEM is branding. Branding can be simply put as a "promise" or how the company is perceived by its customers. Google wishes to be the world's information conduit, Facebook is a communications conduit, and Amazon.com is a commerce conduit. Each of these firms has a clear idea of what and who it is and relates that information to the outside world. Branding is important because brand equity is the value of our firm to the outside world.

---

[9]P. Kireyev, K. Pauwels, and S. Gupta. "Do display ads influence search? Attribution and dynamics in online advertising," *International Journal of Research in Marketing* 33, no. 3, pp. 475–90.

[10]Crestodina. 2014. "Social Medai and SEO Smackdown! [Infographic]," *SEO & Content Marketing, Social Media.* http://www.orbitmedia.com/blog/social-media-seo/?utm_source=June12-newsletter&utm_medium=email&utm_campaign=seo-social-media, (accessed October 13, 2019).

For non-Internet-only monoliths, the challenge becomes integrating the brand promise not only with the firm's offline communications but online as well. In fact, it is my personal belief that branding is more important now that we are so reliant on the Internet to achieve our marketing objectives. There are many ways to reinforce our brands online: search, social media, mobile communications, e-mail, and so on. Each of these forms of communication must reinforce who we are and how we wish people to perceive our brand.

That is why in this part of the book I focus on search as strategy. Understanding who we are and how people search for us is the most critical aspect of our digital marketing management process. Search engines such as Google give acknowledgment to branding efforts. You may have noticed that when you type in a product you are searching for, the name of a large retailer like Amazon and Walmart comes up first, with specialty firms sometimes not showing up until the second page of the search results. The reason is that Google's algorithms give special attention to strong brands because they are trying to "cut through the clutter" on the Internet and provide searchers something of value.

Branding as a concept can be elusive to those who seek to quantify their digital marketing efforts but we can see the results on SERPs. As noted above, Google's algorithms give special attention to strong brands for a variety of reasons. Small companies need to work even harder than large companies to build their brand. Starting with a clear story, telling that story through related content through online channels will increase the chances of having a strong brand. A strong brand will in turn rank highly in search results.[11]

What to Do Next after Chapter 4

1. Using Google Trends, keywordtool.io, and tools such as the Google Ads Keyword Planner, develop a list of keywords that might relate to your company and/or your brand. Be as specific as possible.

---

[11]J.W. Maxx Solutions. 2017. "Personal Online Reputation Management Helps the Way You Look Online." https://jwmaxxsolutions.com/personal-reputation-management/, (accessed October 13, 2019).

2. Group the keywords into categories that might relate to a specific advertising campaign for either Facebook or Google search.

3. Put it all together: Develop ad groups for your campaigns and develop a sample ad for one of your ad groups (if using an ad platform other than Google, still organize your ads into groupings). Make sure the keywords you choose are reflected on your website to also optimize organic search.

Discussion Questions

Discussion 4.1: Relate the discussion on SEM to your product or company. Using one or two specific product lines, do some research for a hypothetical paid search campaign using Google Trends, the Keyword Planner, or another tool. List the company, new product, at least five keywords, and how/why you selected them.

Discussion 4.2: What are the most impactful elements of a website in terms of optimizing a site for organic search? What about paid search?

Glossary

Algorithm: A fancy term for how search engines decide which pages to display for a given search.

CPC: Cost per click, the total amount paid from the ad auction divided by the number of clicks on the ad.

Conversion: A desired action on the part of the customer as a result of your marketing efforts.

Index server: Stores information previously categorized in a search query.

Natural search: What shows up in a search on a search engine, non-paid advertising.

Organic search: Another term for natural search.

PPC: Pay per click, a pricing method for online advertising where we are charged an amount every time a user clicks on our ad.

Query: User-initiated search term.

SEM: Search engine marketing, including both PPC and SEO.

SEO: Search engine optimization, also known as natural or organic search.

SERP: Search engine results page. The SERP is what is shown when we type an inquiry into a search engine. It typically displays both paid and unpaid search results.

Spiders: Also known as "robots"; programs that "crawl" the web and follow every link or piece of data they see and bring them back to the index server.

CHAPTER 5

E-mail Marketing

How E-mail Marketing Fits into Digital Marketing

To discuss how e-mail marketing fits into digital marketing, it is useful to return to Figure 1.1 which illustrates the company's marketing strategy and objectives central to digital marketing and then e-mail, search, social, and web/mobile design as the four foundations of the digital marketing delivery mix. All of these elements of the digital marketing delivery mix should relate to a firm's overall marketing strategy and objectives. These are the primary areas where the company wants to focus on developing digital marketing competencies because they all work together.

So the reason that these channels are foundational is that they work to produce results. Of course, as stated above, before beginning any digital marketing campaign, managers should carefully consider the overall strategy of the organization and the brand positioning strategy, that is, the target market, the products offered, the product category, and the point of differentiation. Without a strong strategic background, all marketing efforts lack focus and are less effective.

Assuming the strategy is in place, the subsequent marketing campaigns that are run on digital platforms should work in tandem. For example, the website should be optimized for organic search in terms of the title tag, appropriate keywords, and user intent, and point the user to sites for social interaction. In turn, search and social media should also work together. One way to ensure they are integrated is to monitor social media channels to understand how to optimize paid and organic search, as discussed in Chapter 4.

E-mail marketing can be integrated with other platforms of digital marketing quite easily. We can include icons on our e-mails pointing customers to social media or back to our websites. Including social media connection information and forwarding capabilities on e-mails can also increase the reach of communications.

There are a number of other ways to make sure e-mail campaigns are integrated with social media.[1] In social media platforms, we can ask customers to give us their contact information in exchange for some specific offers. It is a good practice to use e-mail to send out social media updates and solicit permission for e-mail addresses from customers not only on your website but on social media as well. Once people are on the site, collect customer e-mail addresses and continue to communicate with them effectively. Therefore, as a strategic element of the digital marketing delivery mix, e-mail fits into the scheme of customer retention and service as well as acquisition.

The most effective marketers look at all four foundations of digital delivery and their website design and see how they can work together in an integrated fashion to produce results. Dreamfield's Pasta, which provides a type of pasta targeted toward diabetics (allegedly low carb), is a good example of this type of integrated digital campaign across channels. The company has a high price point, a unique point of difference, and uses this information with a strong grasp of digital channel communication.[2] The video link below describes how this one company clearly understands its unique differentiating point and leverages it across all delivery channels.[3] By understanding its customers and which channels they use, the company created a highly effective cross-channel campaign, using e-mail as its lynchpin. Similarly, Toyota received an award for its e-mail marketing campaign, which drove 70,000 visitors to engage on its website with a simple e-mail directing customers to a microsite (a landing page specific to a campaign) and a follow-on e-mail.[4]

---

[1] Berger. 2013. "Email Marketing + Social Media = A Winning Combination," *Blog.* http://www.business2community.com/email-marketing/email-marketing-social-media-winning-combination-0676745, (accessed October 19, 2019).

[2] M. Roberts and D. Zahay. 2013. *Internet Marketing: Integrating Online and Offline Strategies* (Mason, OH: South –Western Cengage Learning), pp. 177-78.

[3] HyperDrive. 2018. "HyperDrive Hacks Into What Pasta Lovers Really Want!," *Blog.* https://hyperdrivei.com/Clients/dreamfields/case-studies/healthy-hacks-2018, (accessed October 19, 2019).

[4] Dealer Marketing Magazine. 2018. http://www.dealermarketing.com/outsell-and-dspluss-toyota-ch-r-launch-campaign-honored-with-coveted-industry-awards/, (accessed October 13, 2019).

E-mail Marketing as the Unsung Hero
of the Digital Age

E-mail marketing provided the link between campaigns for Dreamfield's and Toyota as it has for many other companies. In many ways, e-mail marketing is the unsung "hero" or "workhorse" of the digital age. The reasons for this statement are many. First, e-mail was the first tool that really allowed companies to take advantage of the interactivity of the Internet in marketing. Using e-mail technology powered by customer data, we could identify those customers most likely to respond to an offer, send a targeted offer, and track the results of the campaigns as well as other statistics. Another reason e-mail continues to be the unsung hero of the digital age is that it does a lot of the work of digital marketing. Although e-mail is not a glamorous technology, it is a powerful one. E-mail technologies are used throughout the customer relationship management process—from e-mails confirming purchases, to follow-on newsletters and promotions, e-mail is a vital tool throughout the customer experience. In fact, in a report from ExactTarget on the State of Marketing in 2014, 88 percent of marketers reported that they use e-mail marketing technology, with 58 percent of them planning to increase their budgets in this area.[5] In business-to-business applications, 93 percent of marketers use e-mail, particularly to distribute content.[6]

Another reason e-mail marketing can be considered the unsung hero of digital marketing is that e-mail marketing was the first digital marketing technology to be used over the Internet that took advantage of the interactivity of the Internet. Prior to the widespread adoption of e-mail as a digital marketing technique, marketers had primarily focused on the use of display advertising. In fact, e-mail has evolved from a broadcast mechanism to a permission-based channel to a true engagement channel.

The thinking in the beginning was that the computer looked like a small television screen, so let's advertise on it! What marketers failed to take into account was that the Internet provided consumers with much

[5]ExactTarget. 2014. "State of Marketing," *Report.* https://brandcdn.exacttarget.com/sites/exacttarget/files/2014stateofmarketing.pdf, (accessed October 14, 2019).
[6]Content Marketing Institute. 2017. "B2B Content Marketing," *PDF.* https://contentmarketinginstitute.com/wp-content/uploads/2016/09/2017_B2B_Research_FINAL.pdf, (accessed January 9, 2020).

more control and the desire for control over their content. In order for an ad to be seen, much more work had to be done on the part of the marketer. Click-through rates (CTRs) on display ads were high and then rapidly fell to a similar range for direct mail, 2 to 3 percent or less. What was needed was a way to get the consumer's attention and also to take advantage of what makes digital marketing unique. Digital media allow for interactivity, the use of customer information, and immediate response in the form of a conversation. Digital media also involve the customer in the marketing process and enable engagement.

E-mail marketing is well suited to the digital age. E-mail marketing provides for there to be interactivity because the consumer can respond and his or her preferences can be taken into account in the next communication. E-mail is immediate because, especially with mobile devices, the message can be delivered in a timely manner. E-mail is "involving" because the messages, although brief, can lead to other parts of the Internet and thus draw the consumer into a particular website. E-mail is information-intense because we can use information collected about the consumer in our communications to them via e-mail.

E-mail marketing caught on rapidly because of these features that are related to the interactivity of digital marketing. However, it was also natural to compare e-mail to traditional forms of direct marketing, particularly direct mail, because of the similarities. The missives were delivered to the customer's inbox (instead of physical mailbox), could be addressed to the customer specifically, and could contain a targeted offer.

However, there were several key differences between the two communications channels. E-mail is faster, cheaper, and more effective than direct mail. E-mail is faster because offers can be assembled quickly without having to wait for the print production process. It is cheaper because again there is no need to print and mail communications. It is more effective because we can quickly determine customer response and change the next offer to increase response rate. In fact, although we used to have to wait three weeks for direct mail response, the time was shortened to three days and today, most responses are garnered within the first 24 hours after the e-mail is sent. So, e-mail is seen as more effective than direct mail because response rates are higher and because we can quickly change our offers and parameters and gauge results. E-mail statistics vary by industry, country, and quality of the list used. However, in spite of the negative publicity that e-mail has received and its association with spam, unique open rates (unique individuals who open the e-mail) are hovering at about 21 percent[7] and CTRs at about 2.6 percent,[8] quite acceptable metrics. Although open rates have declined a bit, depending on the study, overall CTRs are remaining relatively consistent. Most Western and European countries have similar statistics. The current unsubscribe rate is about 0.17 percent.[9] The bottom line is that users still open e-mails that are relevant to them.

E-mail as a Branding Tool

What has really put e-mail marketing on the map is not only the access to measurement but the ability to integrate with other marketing channels. The integration of the four foundations of the digital marketing delivery mix—search, social, e-mail, and mobile—with website design is made easier through e-mail marketing. We can put links to our social sites on e-mail and put keyword-rich terminology on our e-mail messages and our website.

As discussed above, a typical scenario is to drive people to the Facebook site or other social media sites via e-mail or the website, collect customer information, and continue ongoing communications that way.

E-mail can reinforce our brand image as well, by producing a consistent message to the customer. Branding, as illustrated in Chapter 4, takes many forms on the Internet. In its most basic terms, branding is our promise to the customer about what value our product will deliver. Whether it be cleaner floors or efficient computer software, branding is an

---

[7]MailChimp. 2019. "Average Email Campaign Stats of MailChimp Customers by Industry." https://mailchimp.com/resources/email-marketing-benchmarks/, (accessed January 9, 2020).

[8]Campaign Monitor. 2019. "Ultimate Email Marketing Benchmarks for 2019: By Industry & Day." https://www.campaignmonitor.com/resources/guides/email-marketing-benchmarks/, (accessed October 13, 2019).

[9]Campaign Monitor. 2019. "Ultimate Email Marketing Benchmarks for 2019: By Industry & Day." https://www.campaignmonitor.com/resources/guides/email-marketing-benchmarks/, (accessed October 13, 2019).

important aspect of customer communication. In fact, in an increasingly fragmented world of customer communications, branding can be considered the way to "break through the clutter" of the consumer inbox to create a unique and special message to which the consumer will respond.

Typically, the e-mail is used as a promotional message. However, e-mails can be used effectively in a content marketing strategy to reinforce a brand image. For example, a local Chicago website development company[10] uses bimonthly web posts to increase traffic to its website and reinforce its brand image. The company wishes to be known for its image as a leading purveyor of website development expertise. The blog posts are promoted on the website and customers and prospects are encouraged to subscribe to the system. The blog posts are then e-mailed out each month to encourage readership. The e-mail format also makes it easier for the posts to "go viral" and reach a larger audience.

However, some marketers indicate that they do not believe digital marketing has delivered as a branding vehicle. Gartner Group indicates that social, mobile, analytics, and e-commerce are the most frequently recognized tools of digital marketing. We have focused on the four foundations of the digital marketing delivery mix (search, social, e-mail, mobile) supporting our central website design. It is not at all surprising that this set of delivery platforms would not be considered effective branding tools. These tools can reinforce a brand image but not create a brand image. In general, the most effective way to build a brand image is still through various forms of advertising, whether traditional or digital.[11]

E-mail as a Retention Tool

If overall, e-mail is faster, cheaper, more effective, and more easily measured than direct mail and effective in brand-building, it is no surprise that e-mail as a digital channel caught on quickly. Marketers rapidly

[10]Orbit Media Studios. 2014. http://orbitmedia.com, (accessed October 13, 2019).

[11]Marketing Charts Staff. 2014. "Few Digital Marketers Feel that Digital has Delivered as a Branding Vehicle," *MC Website.* http://www.marketingcharts.com/wp/online/few-digital-marketers-feel-that-digital-has-delivered-as-a-branding-vehicle-43308/?utm_campaign=newsletter&utm_source=mc&utm_medium=textlink, (accessed October 13, 2019).

realized, however, that customers did not appreciate receiving e-mails from those whom they did not have a prior business relationship with. Seth Godin[12] coined the term "permission marketing" around this time and e-mail marketers adopted the concept of different levels of permission. Approximately 80 percent of business professionals list e-mail as their top retention tool, outpacing other communications channels by over two to one.[13]

To further understand e-mail marketing as a retention tool, let's take a closer look at the distinction of what digital marketing is by examining the Gartner Group definition and seeing how e-mail might fit into the scheme. Gartner defines digital marketing as a "set of techniques, enabled by technology, which allows marketing to improve its processes to engage in a dynamic conversation with people who are influencers and buyers and ultimately target, acquire and retain customers. Digital marketing includes the ability to interactively communicate with customers through electronic channels, such as the Web, e-mail, smart devices such as phones and tablets, and mobile applications."[14]

Therefore, e-mail is a digital technology that allows for a conversation to occur between the buyer and seller. E-mail, although best used for customer retention efforts such as ongoing communications via newsletters and promotions, can be used to target and acquire customers. Because of legal concerns which will be discussed later and the perceived intrusive nature of "spam" e-mails, consumer response to e-mails is better when there is an established relationship. (Parenthetically, the term "spam" came from an old Monty Python skit in which the word was used over and over and did not originate from the product by Hormel).

As we have come to understand through our work so far, companies need to know who they are and develop a clear positioning strategy in

[12]S. Godin. 1999. *Permission Marketing Turning Strangers into Friends, and Friends into Customers* (New York, NY: Simon and Schuster).

[13]Emarsys. 2016. "Adapting to the pace of omnichannel commerce," *PDF*. https://www.emarsys.com/app/uploads/2018/01/eTail-Emarsys-WBR-SMB-Report.pdf, (January 9, 2020).

[14]Gartner. 2013. "Key Findings from U.S. Digital Marketing Spending Survey, 2013," *Gartner for Marketing Leaders*. https://www.gartner.com/technology/research/digital-marketing/digital-marketing-spend-report.jsp, (accessed October 13, 2019).

order to begin their digital marketing campaigns. The next step is then to develop a clear objective for the particular digital technology. These objectives may be set using the customer lifecycle. As the customer life-cycle indicates, e-mail is best used as a retention tool. The reason is that e-mail that is expected is more likely to be opened and read by current customers.

In fact, as indicated by the four foundations of the digital marketing delivery mix, e-mail does not work alone. Search, social, and mobile/web design are all important to digital marketers and can be used by e-mail mar-keters. In fact, e-mail mobile and loyalty are all intertwined. As with every aspect of digital marketing, mobile marketing is having an impact on e-mail marketing. About 46 percent of e-mail opens are on mobile devices.[15]

For example, Rack Room Shoes was able to analyze customer data and then create a permission-based loyalty program for its customers, busy moms. Consumers wanted quick access to their rewards points and so the company created a digital program that was accessible through a mobile application. Reminders were sent by e-mail messages. Customers preferred e-mail messages because of the limited number of text charac-ters. However, e-mails were quite often opened on the mobile platform either before, after, or during the shopping experience. The results in terms of customer loyalty and sales were striking. The company captured 20 percent more of its customers' overall shoe budget (share of wallet). Rack Room Shoes also saw the number of customers spending more than $400 a year increase.[16]

This type of e-mail marketing with permission is highly effective. As e-mail has evolved from broadcast spam to permission to true engage-ment, it has continued to hold a solid place in the digital marketer's list of tools. As noted on the previous page, the highest response rates and other measurements will most likely come from a list of the marketer's current

---

[15]Specht. 2018. "Email Client Market Share Trends for the First Half of 2018." https://litmus.com/blog/email-client-market-share-trends-first-half-of-2018, (accessed January 9, 2020).

[16]Direct Marketing News. n.d. "If Only Engendering Loyalty Was as Easy as Clicking Your Heels," *Multichannel Marketing*. https://www.dmnews.com/marketing-channels/multi-omnichannel/news/13057161/if-only-engendering-loyalty-was-as-easy-as-clicking-your-heels, (accessed October 13, 2019).

customers or "house list" because those customers have purchased before and are familiar with the product.

Figure 5.1 illustrates the different levels of permission—opt-out, opt-in, confirmed opt-in, and double opt-in. Each one requires a higher level of commitment from the customer. Therefore, the tool is not really optimal for customer acquisition. If we think about the customer acquisition and relationship continuum, we would see that e-mail is best for customer retention and service. E-mails that are permission-based and use information that the customer has given us to develop tailored communications have the best results.

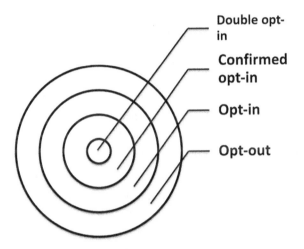

Double opt-in

Confirmed opt-in

Opt-in

Opt-out

Figure 5.1 Layers of permission

The different types of permission in e-mail marketing are opt-out, opt-in, confirmed opt-in, and double opt-in as shown in Figure 5.1. Opt-out is the lowest level of permission, when a box is checked on an e-mail and the consumer must "uncheck" the box to not receive future e-mails. In opt-in, the box is unchecked and must be checked to start receiving communications. With confirmed opt-in we send another e-mail to confirm intention and with double opt-in we send yet another e-mail to confirm the consumer's wishes. Although response rates might drop off with double opt-in e-mails, the quality of customers is usually quite high.

In opt-out, we ask the customer to do something so as not to receive future information from us. In opt-in the opposite is true; we ask the customer to *do* something to continue receiving communications from us. In confirmed opt-in, we send a communication that tells the customer what has happened and remind them that they will be receiving future communication. In the highest form of permission, the double opt-in, we ask the customer to reconfirm their original intention to opt in.

E-mail response is measured by CTR, which is the number of e-mails opened divided by the number of e-mails delivered. E-mails that are not delivered are said to have "bounced," with a "hard" bounce being an undeliverable e-mail and a "soft" bounce being an e-mail that could not be delivered at that time. Perhaps a better measure of e-mail performance is the click to open rate (CTOR), which is the number of unique opens divided by the number of e-mails delivered. Unique opens are important in terms of tracking performance because these individuals may be interacting with us more than once and unique opens mean they are not double counted.

All these analytical metrics must reinforce the major goal of e-mail marketing campaigns and help to integrate the e-mail program with our customer relationship and retention programs and to create engagement. There is no doubt that e-mail marketing has become a valuable tool for communication. E-mail has become known primarily as a tool for customer retention rather than acquisition. The delivery platform is suited not just to promotions but to ongoing customer communication for customer retention such as newsletters. In fact, it might be said that e-mail marketing is a powerful tool of the digital marketing age. The tool has consistently provided a way for firms to communicate with their customers and open rates and CTRs have remained surprisingly consistent over the years as well. With 50 percent of the population starting their day with e-mail and with mobile communications putting e-mail at our fingertips all the time, the tool has become invaluable for marketers.

E-mail Marketing as a Process

In general, a fully developed process also helps our e-mail marketing efforts (see Figure 5.2). As the process below indicates, we start with the data we may already have on our customers. We analyze our current database and segment it and analyze the response rates, if any. We then create, execute, and measure our campaign and use those results to create the next iteration.

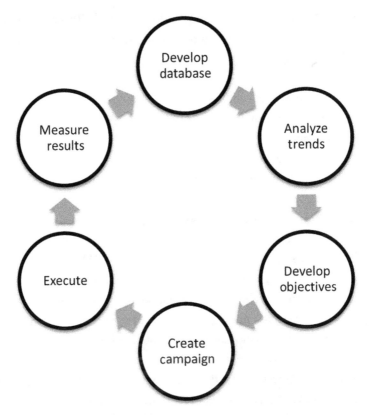

Figure 5.2 E-mail marketing campaign process

If we are building a database from scratch, we need to find ways to incentivize our customer to provide e-mail addresses to us. We can collect e-mail addresses through online registration on our website, face-to-face events, offline advertising, or through social media. List brokers will also provide lists of customers that have agreed to opt in to e-mail offers from companies that they don't know. Typically, we don't acquire the e-mail address unless they respond to the offer. As noted above, sending e-mails to individuals without permission, at least in the form of a prior relationship, is not recommended, not in the least because it does not provide the best results. Fortunately, there are many ways to obtain these permission-based e-mails to avoid the perception of spam.

In fact, the lack of permission in e-mail marketing led in 2003 to the federal legislation known as the "Controlling the Assault of Non-Solicited Pornography and Marketing Act" (CAN-SPAM). This important piece of legislation was intended to curb abuse by spammers and those who "phish" for sensitive information via e-mail. This e-mail legislation applies to acquisition or promotional e-mails and says they must have the following:

- Valid from e-mail address
- Valid reply to e-mail
- Street address
- Unsubscribe provision
- Be clearly recognizable as advertising

CAN-SPAM has become so well-recognized that many marketers who do not need to do so, such as those sending relational or transactional e-mails, still adhere to many of the CAN-SPAM rules. A good way to tell if an e-mail is official is to look for the valid reply address, street address, and unsubscribe provision. So, part of our e-mail marketing process is generally finding a way to adhere to federal legislation.[17] In 2019, the Federal Trade Commission voted to keep the law as is with no changes. However, other regulations, such as the European Union General Data Protection (GDPR) rules and the California Consumer Privacy Act (CCPA), have brought consumer data privacy to the fore and have made e-mail marketers more aware of how they treat sensitive customer information. Canada also has special legislation regulating the use of email and marketers sending email communications to that country need to abide by that legislation.

Often, we use an e-mail service provider (ESP) to help manage the database and our marketing metrics. ESPs typically use hundreds of different offers and are able to track them individually. Other reasons to use ESPs such as ExactTarget Marketing Cloud Services or Mail Chimp is to help get e-mails delivered through Internet service providers (ISPs) and not marked as spam, aid in tracking and measurement, and easily integrate with social media and other campaigns. ESPs also help keep us compliant with CAN-SPAM by making it easy to do so.

---

[17]DMA. 2003. "The CAN-SPAM Act of 2003," *JPG*. http://thedma.org/wp-content/uploads/CAN-SPAM-Act.jpg, (accessed October 13, 2019).

Once we have the database in place, we can analyze the data and use segmentation and persona marketing (Chapters 3 and 6) to refine our offers. Using ESPs, we can provide dynamic content, changing offers, photographs, links, and other parts of our e-mail according to the target segment. This dynamic content capability allows companies to use personalization, as discussed in an earlier chapter, to great advantage. Customers respond to personalized messages, although some research indicates that caution is needed. Customers can perceive communications as "too much, too soon," and the relationship needs to be developed slowly over a period of time before extensive personalization is used.[18] This situation highlights the fact that e-mail marketing is best used as a retention tool.

Effective E-mail Design and Offers

Whatever the objective, the e-mail marketing campaign must be planned. Typically, we decide on the objective of the campaign and the target audience and create a viable list from which to work. We then create compelling copy and a subject line for the e-mail. Critical to effective design is what is known as a "call to action." The call to action is a principle from direct marketing that simply refers to what the company wants the consumer to *do* upon receiving the communication. Typical calls to action include asking for a purchase or to download information or asking for a customer response or review. Good calls to action should be specific and include a time deadline. Without urgency, customers will not have an incentive to react. These principles can also be used effectively in writing paid search advertising. Effective "action" words include the following:

- Buy
- Order
- Call
- Visit

---

[18]T. White, D.L. Zahay, H. Thorbjornsen, and S. Shavitt. 2008. "Getting Too Personal: Reactance to Highly Personalized Email Solicitations," *Marketing Letters* 19, no. 1, pp. 39-50.

- Download
- Read
- Print

One effective call-to-action word from direct marketing that is not so effective in direct e-mail marketing is the word "free." Highly effective offline, in print media, the word "free" will often be a red flag to ISPs, as action is not the only principle of direct marketing that can be applied in e-mail marketing. In fact, many direct marketing principles are now being applied in e-mail marketing, search, social, and website design.[19] One of these principles is A/B testing as noted in Chapter 4. In this approach we test one particular offer, known as the "control", against something which has been changed to see which is most effective. Multivariate testing involves testing multiple aspects of the e-mail at once to see which combinations produce the best results.

The detailed process of e-mail design is beyond the scope of this book. However, making sure that your e-mail is "above the fold" and uses the "golden triangle" principle from website design is another way to ensure a higher response rate. Making sure that the offer is clear and can be easily found and responded to is another way to increase response. As in website design, principles from behavioral psychology can also apply.

E-mail Metrics

In general, in designing e-mails we can put in links that can then be tracked and analyzed and these can provide valuable information on our customers' interests and background. We can also use the results from e-mail campaigns and site visits to conduct e-mail retargeted campaigns. Retargeting e-mails can help move those who have visited our site and not purchased or perhaps abandoned their shopping cart to get closer to

---

[19]D. Zahay and B. Massey. 2013. "Everything I Needed to Know about CRO I Learned from Direct Response Marketers," *Slideshare*. https://www.slideshare.net/ bmassey/what-we-can-learn-from-direct-marketers-by-brian-massey-and-debra-zahay-23117583?utm_source=slideshow&utm_medium=ssemail&utm_%20 campaign=upload_digest, (accessed October 13, 2019).

purchase. In addition, ESPs will provide us with a number of key marketing metrics for e-mail marketing. A few of these metrics are stated below:

- Open rate: Percent of e-mails opened
- Bounce rate: Percent of e-mails undelivered (a "hard bounce" is a bad e-mail address; a "soft bounce" is one that is temporarily undeliverable)
- Unsubscribe rate: Percent of customers unsubscribing from our offer
- What links were clicked
- CTR: The number of clicks the e-mail generated divided by number of e-mails sent
- Forwards/Saves/Prints: Other measurements of activity on the e-mail

The specific e-mail metrics that a company uses depends on particular campaign objectives. Hopefully you have an idea of how to develop an e-mail campaign using permission principles and some idea of how to measure the results.

What to Do Next after Chapter 5

1. Imagine you are creating a campaign for a company or service. Determine where you are going to get your list of e-mail contacts; if you have responses from prior e-mails, consider those. Which do you think will be most effective and why?
2. Develop a list of more detailed objectives for an e-mail campaign based on the customer acquisition and relationship management process (Figure 1.8).
3. Design an e-mail for one of the campaign objectives that you have defined. You can use a free e-mail marketing service for the design or just paper and pencil. Who is the audience? What is the call to action, the timing? How will you measure results?

Discussion Questions

Discussion 5.1: Think about e-mail communications from marketers, perhaps some that you have received yourself. What makes them interesting and worth your time to open and read? Do you ever take any action as a result of the e-mails? Why or why not?

Discussion 5.2: If you were running an e-mail marketing campaign for your own or another company, what would be the most important metrics you would use and why?

Discussion 5.3: What are the main benefits of using an ESP? Do you think it is advisable to use such a service or to send the e-mails out on a personal or company e-mail address?

Discussion 5.4: Explain the concept of permission marketing. Does this concept relate to marketing beyond e-mail marketing? How?

Glossary

A/B split test: Testing two treatments of a website, an ad, e-mail, or direct mail communication with one modification to see which treatment is more effective.

Bounce rate: Percent of e-mails undelivered (a hard bounce is a bad e-mail address; a soft bounce is one that is temporarily undeliverable).

Call to action: What you are asking the customer to do (usually by when).

CAN-SPAM: Stands for Controlling the Assault of Non-Solicited Pornography and Marketing Act; regulates unwanted e-mails; only applies if there is no prior relationship.

Click-through rate (CTR): The number of clicks the e-mail generated divided by the number of e-mails sent.

CTOR or CTO (Click to open): Number of unique opens divided by the number of e-mails delivered.

Open rate: Number of emails opened divided by number delivered.

Permission marketing: Asking someone to opt in or getting them to consent to receiving marketing communication.

Unsubscribe rate: Percentage of customers unsubscribing from a particular offer.

CHAPTER 6

Content Marketing, Social Media and the Role of Mobile

Social Media Marketing Defined

The next delivery mechanism for digital marketing communications we will discuss is social media marketing. Social media marketing should be distinguished from social media platforms themselves. Social media marketing (SMM) as a process is the business use of social media channels to understand customers and engage them in such a way that leads to the achievement of ultimate marketing and business goals. Therefore, the ultimate goal of SMM is to use social media tools to reach a particular target consumer and to foster engagement, social sharing, and advocacy among the customer base. There are various forms of social media such as blogs, chat rooms, social networking sites, podcasts, and so on, as shown in Figure 6.1. Each platform has its own place in a SMM campaign, depending on where the customer is and the company's strategy, website, and brand objectives. However, while social media spend is increasing by double digits, still only about 20 percent of marketers say they can quantitatively demonstrate the impact of these marketing efforts.[1] Importantly, this trend has been the same in recent years.[2]

---

[1]LYFE Marketing. 2019. "5 Easy Steps on How to Measure Your Social Media ROI." https://www.lyfemarketing.com/blog/social-media-roi/, (accessed January 9, 2020).
[2]M. Christine. 2019. The CMO Survey.

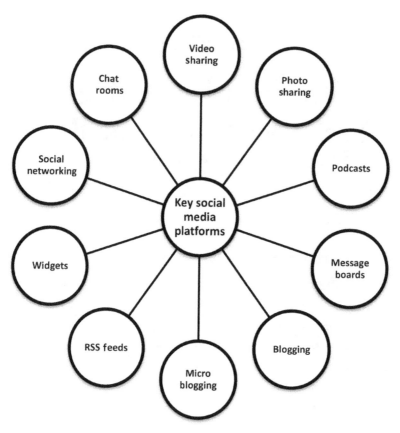

Figure 6.1 The proliferation of social platforms

How Social Media Marketing Relates to Content Marketing

Taking a step back, we need to look at social media in the context of content marketing. We also need to take a further step back and look at content marketing in the context of the brand story. Once we have decided our positioning strategy and developed the brand story, we need to decide what content will help reinforce that story. For a university, for example, it might be success stories of recent graduates. Storytelling in marketing is how to get consumers to better relate to our brand because human beings are wired to respond to stories and retain that information.[3] For example, Red Bull has a prizewinning content marketing program. Their content goes beyond their product to the types of activities their customers engage in, such as biking, surfing, and extreme sports, and tells their personal stories. The site also features products of interest such as Internet watches. Content is disseminated on the website and through social media platforms, blogs, and so on.

Content marketing is also important in developing search terms on the website that reinforce the brand story. So, as shown in Figure 6.2, we first develop our brand story, then decide what type of content will reinforce our brand, and then how that content will be repurposed on various channels. Content marketing is more important than ever before because of its relevance to both paid and organic search. In paid search, the algorithms are looking for relevant content on a page to serve an ad and in organic search they are looking for deep and meaningful content to serve a page in the search results.

Previously we talked about the power of networks which means that information on the Internet spreads rapidly. Putting networks together with the power of a long-standing marketing concept, word of mouth, means that marketers hope to influence the word of mouth about the product positively. Marketers do so by cultivating key social "influencers" who can be identified through SMM software tools such as Radian6 (the most popular). For example, Braun marketed its new coffee maker by identifying key influencers and getting them to blog about the product and share information online. Recently it initiated a similar campaign for its CoolTec shaver.[4] The company used 500 "brand ambassadors" to spread the word about the product on various social media platforms.

[3]LYFE Marketing. 2019. "5 Easy Steps on How to Measure Your Social Media ROI." https://www.lyfemarketing.com/blog/social-media-roi/, (accessed January 16, 2020).
[4]What Works in Youth HIV. 2018. "Strategies for Social Marketing Campaigns." https://www.whatworksinyouthhiv.org/strategies/social-media-and-marketing-strategies/strategies-social-marketing-campaigns, (accessed October 13, 2019).

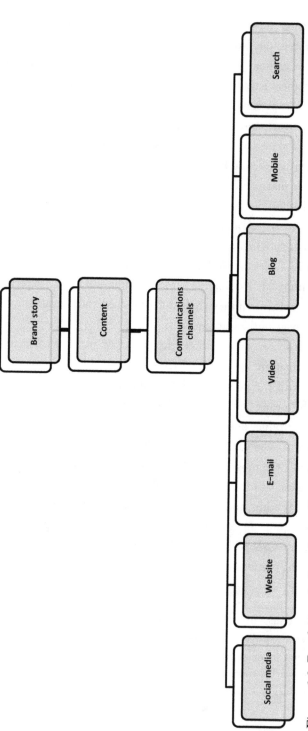

Figure 6.2 Developing the brand story through content

Successful Social Media Campaigns

Successful social media campaigns run the gamut and there is no one key to success. If a company tries to make a campaign "go viral," it cannot be done. This is where the marketplace has really taken hold of the digital marketing process. Some examples of successful campaigns that have taken off online include the "Old Spice" video campaign, both offline and on YouTube, which has transformed the brand from an "old guy" one into a hip brand used by young people.

Often even business-to-business companies, which have lagged behind business-to-customer companies in terms of SMM usage, can make use of humor to create engagement. One example of such an approach is Sungard's "Zombie Apocalypse" guide to using its protection services in case of the coming imaginary Zombie attack. Content marketing strategies are critical today in B2B demand generation where it is estimated that 57 percent of the purchase decision has been made before the customer even touches the client. Applications such as Shopkick have made the process of shopping itself a social function, with users getting points for entering certain stores.

Paid, Earned, Owned, and Shared Media

When thinking about implementing a SMM campaign, we categorize social media across all four types of media channels—paid, earned, owned, and shared media (Figure 6.3). It is possible to pay for media by advertising on social sites or sponsoring blog posts and tweets (these sponsorship opportunities must be identified as such). Companies can own different platforms such as their own blogs and social media accounts. Firms can also earn attention when videos, blog posts, and other types of information go "viral" through social media. Shared content occurs when the company and consumer co-create content, often on social media platforms, as when a brand such as Doritos® invites customers to create advertisements for the product or when customers spontaneously create such content. The most cherished content is that which is earned by the firm and that which is shared with the customer because that content has the ability to create long-lasting impressions and to "go viral," creating awareness and brand loyalty that is impossible to purchase.

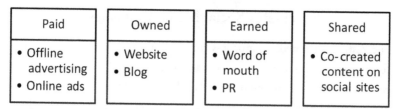

Paid	Owned	Earned	Shared
• Offline advertising • Online ads	• Website • Blog	• Word of mouth • PR	• Co-created content on social sites

Figure 6.3 Types of media and examples

Social Media and Engagement

At this point it is reasonable to talk about what customer engagement (CE) means. Brodie et al.[5] defined it as "a psychological state that occurs by virtue of interactive, co-creative customer experiences with a focal agent/object (e.g., a brand) in focal service relationships. It occurs under a specific set of context-dependent conditions generating differing CE levels; and exists as a dynamic, iterative process within service relationships that co-create value. CE plays a central role in a nomological network governing service relationships in which other relational concepts (e.g., involvement, loyalty) are antecedents and/or consequences in iterative CE processes. It is a multidimensional concept subject to a context- and/or stakeholder-specific expression of relevant cognitive, emotional, and/or behavioral dimensions."

In other words, CE is both a state and a process. When customers interact in a process that is co-creative with a brand, they can be said to be in a state of engagement. However, engagement is also a process which can be used to develop deeper customer loyalty, for example, which then, iteratively, engenders engagement.

Social media platforms that allow for sharing and creation of content are therefore prime candidates for companies to use for CE. Right now, the top five social media networking platforms used by marketers in terms of unique monthly visitors are Facebook, YouTube (Google), Instagram, Twitter, and WhatsApp.[6] However, Pinterest, Reddit, Tumblr, and Flickr

[5]R. Brodie, L. Hollebeek, B. Juric, and A. Illic, "Customer Engagement: Conceptual Domain, Fundamental Propositions, and Implications for Research," *Journal of Service Research* 14, no. 3, pp. 252-71.

[6]eBiz|MBA. "Top 15 Most Popular Social Networking Sites January 2020," *Website.* http://www.ebizmba.com/articles/social-networking-websites, (accessed January 9, 2020).

have more influence than WhatsApp. Instagram, with its ability to share photos quickly, is quite popular not only among millennials but also among those marketing visual products. TikTok, a platform for sharing short-form mobile videos popular among Generation Z, is growing rapidly. The bookmarking site Reddit.com has also become popular with marketers of late. As of the time of writing this, several new platforms were launching and who knows which ones will take off and provide real potential for marketers.

After all, the rule of thumb in SMM is to "fish where the fish are;"[7] so if your target customer is on a particular site, it is useful to monitor that site. For example, if you run a restaurant, Yelp might be a good choice. If you are marketing to businesses, you might choose LinkedIn as a platform. Facebook has been found to be a good source of brand-building for consumer brands, whereas Twitter can be used for both B2B and B2C applications.

Social media influencers are often paid to promote or mention specific products in social media. These influencers have access to targeted audiences and marketers often find it more expedient to use an influencer than to develop the audience on their own. Some influencers, like Lil Miquela, are computer-generated and reflect a broader trend for advertisers to have more control over influencer audiences and avoid some of the legal requirements for influencers to disclose when they are paid for promotions.

Personas can be used in social media just as they are used for website development. When creating personas for social media we take into account the social media platforms which the persona might frequent and their level of engagement. Many B2B companies, such as IBM, create their own social media platforms for private use, often known as "white label" networks. On these private networks, the company's staff can share information among themselves and/or users. Sometimes these private networks are used for new product development efforts and the company wishes to keep the information outside of the public domain. Forrester Research has an online version of its Technographics ladder

[7] J. Zimmerman. 2012. *Web Marketing for Dummies* (Hoboken, NJ: John Wiley & Sons).

which demonstrates how social media usage changes across various age groups and gender. You can use the tool to see creators, conversationalists, collectors, critics, joiners, spectators, and inactives change across these boundaries.[8] As the Forrester ladder shows, only about a quarter of the population creates content on social media, whereas three-quarters of us are spectators on social media. This means that for engagement we are not going to be able to get everyone in a high state of engagement. We do, however, need to take our audience into account and provide content that people will want to read and share.

The trick in SMM is to not just talk to the customer but to get them to comment and share on what is relevant to them. After a rapport has been established, it is fine to ask customers what they want directly. Another way of finding out what they are thinking about is to use some of the monitoring tools mentioned in this chapter.

Planning, Monitoring, and Measuring

Planning the social media campaign is critical to success. Usually we consider that the steps in social media planning are:

1. Listen to the customer
2. Communicate with the customer
3. Foster engagement with the customer
4. Work toward collaboration with the customer

We have had an example of a listening tool in Google Trends. In listening we want to monitor both trends and sentiment (positive or negative) around topics and firms. An example of collaboration known as crowdsourcing is the Threadless.com site where users submit t-shirt designs for which they are given a small fee if the user community votes that the design is used in t-shirts to be sold to the public by Threadless. Other types of collaboration include making changes to products and

---

[8]ToolsHero. 2014. "Social Technographics Profile." https://www.toolshero.com/social-media/social-technographics-profile/, (accessed January 9, 2020).

service processes as a result of customer input or encouraging customers to make videos about the product that are shared on the web.

Hootsuite™ is the market leader in the category of tools that allows for monitoring of social media content and engaging in social media discussions. The company offers an online certification program and a university program that helps professors train students in social media. Tools such as Hootsuite™ allow for scheduling of posts in advance, which can allow for the implementation of a content marketing calendar on social media. In general, a calendar should be used that crosses media so that messages can be controlled and coordinated across channels. The calendar should be based on the objectives for the SMM plan, remembering that the customer is also an active participant in that plan, and that engagement must be a stated objective. A sample content marketing plan is shown in Figure 6.4.

Message objective	Media	Timing	Message content	Responsibility
Branding	E-mail	First of the month	Reinforce brand tag line	E-mail marketing team
Tips and techniques	Social media (Facebook) Twitter	Twice weekly Twice daily	How to use the product, product updates	Social media team
Promotions	E-mail, social media, website, blogs	Monthly	Discounts, promotions	Marketing assistant
Engagement	Social media Facebook	Twice a year	Games, contests	Social media plan

Figure 6.4 *Sample content marketing plan*

Other tools for monitoring include HubSpot, Sprout Social, BuzzSumo, and Keyhole.[9] Free social listening tools include the free versions of Hootsuite™ and SumAll, as well as free tools offered by vendors such as Google Trends, Google Alerts, Facebook Insights, and Twitter's advanced tools. As with each of the four foundations of the digital

---

[9]Amaresan. 2019. "10 of the best social listening tools to monitor mentions of your brand." https://blog.hubspot.com/service/social-listening-tools, (accessed January 9, 2020).

marketing delivery mix, when we work in social media marketing we need to have a process for putting our plan together and engaging with the customer base in a meaningful way. For example, Hilton Hotels is known for understanding its customers well and providing the right type of pillow in the room at check-in and having customer information at their fingertips. Hilton often engages in social listening to determine customers' specific needs.

Objectives may range from branding to creating advocacy, although direct sales pitches often are perceived negatively by social media users. Although coupons have also been used effectively on social media, the emphasis should be content. Generally, the more content we can share that is useful to our customers, the deeper the brand relationship.

For every social media campaign, there should be tools to measure the success of the campaign. We might measure likes, comments, and shares depending on the objectives of the campaign. To develop proper measurement tools, think about your company and what you might hope to achieve from social media. It is important to take into account how each platform displays your posts and comments. For example, the Facebook EdgeRank algorithm shows the people with which you are most engaged. A small business might not have its posts show up on its users' stream if there has been no prior engagement. The marketing effort might not be effective because not everyone is seeing the posts. Often in social media measurement, we have to determine which platform or application should receive what percent of credit for the final sale online, a process known as attribution.[10]

To have it all work together, content marketing strategies that incorporate social media must be based on relevant keywords. In Chapter 4, I suggested carefully considering the keywords which are most relevant to our efforts. Keywords need to be continually updated and incorporated across all of our content marketing strategy. However, since Google is providing less information on keywords than it used to, it can be difficult to determine which organic search keywords are driving users to

[10]A. Barger and L. Labreque. 2013. "An Integrated Marketing Communications Perspective on Social Media Metrics," *International Journal of Integrated Marketing Communications* 5, no. 1, pp. 64-76.

your site. Google Webmaster tools provides some insight, as can running even a limited paid search campaign, looking at search sources other than Google and seeing which landing pages are being most frequently accessed.[11] It can also be useful to survey customers and see what they continue to access and look at to determine which keywords can be best used on social media and other content to optimize your content marketing strategy.

Combining Mobile and Local (SoLoMo)

If digital, content, and SMM are all about engagement, then mobile marketing is all about engaging with the customer when and where they are ready to make a decision or create engagement. Mobile marketing has arrived, but what is it? While web/mobile design is considered one of the four foundations of the digital marketing delivery mix—search, social, web/mobile design, and e-mail—mobile is not a specific marketing channel. Mobile is a delivery platform upon which digital messages can be conveyed and digital customer interactions can be undertaken and measured. Mobile platforms include smartphones, tablets, and other devices imagined or yet to be imagined (such as Smart Watches and Google Glasses).

Mobile is part of a trend called "SoLoMo" in which marketing is, as the name suggests, social, local, and mobile. This trend is also sometimes called digital convergence because of the coming together of content from many media channels on digital devices.[12] Digital convergence, accessing information on multiple platforms, also includes the "Internet of Things" in which home appliances and other devices not usually considered "smart" are able to be controlled by consumers via various Internet-enabled devices.

---

[11]Dykes. 2013. "How Google's Expanded Search Encryption Impacts Adobe Analytics," *Adobe Blog*. https://theblog.adobe.com/how-googles-expanded-search-encryption-impacts-adobe-analytics, (accessed October 13, 2019).

[12]CCENT. 2014. "About." *Center for Convergence and Emerging Network Technologies Website*. http://ccent.syr.edu/about/.

Integrated SoLoMo

These concepts of SoLoMo are being used to create marketing campaigns that integrate social media, local computing, and mobile devices (Figure 6.5). Often, gaming concepts are integrated as well; gaming is a growing industry. For example, the MINI Getaway was launched on iPhones in Stockholm. The goal was to find and create brand evangelists for the new version of the MINI. Users captured a virtual MINI on their phone and then ran because others within a certain distance could "take" the mini for themselves. The contest went on for several weeks until the last person with a MINI on their iPhone won a real MINI Countryman car. Thousands of people in Stockholm played the game, clogging the streets in the last days of play. Hundreds of thousands of social shares resulted and the marketers claim that a "movement" was created as well.[13] A similar example is the M&M's "find Red" game which involved users in tracking down M&M's Red character on their phones throughout Toronto.[14]

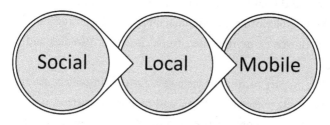

Figure 6.5 *SoLoMo defines digital marketing*

Like any aspect of digital marketing, campaigns and interactions on mobile platforms must be carefully planned and have measureable objectives. With the rapid pace of change in this area, measurement must be continually reassessed.

---

[13]MINI Getaway Stockholm. 2010. "MINI Getaway Stockholm 2010—Case study," *Video.* https://www.youtube.com/watch?v=dt9OlGq3gWU, (accessed October 13, 2019).

[14]Proximity Worldwide. 2011. "M&M's Find Red," *Video.* https://www.youtube.com/watch?v=_pXX277TKzw, (accessed October 13, 2019).

Mobile marketing is also part of a trend called "pervasive computing" in which the marketer can access any customer at any time, over any Internet-enabled device. Not only can e-mails, search, and social media interactions be delivered or take place on mobile devices, but mobile marketing also includes video marketing, QR and barcodes, text messages, display advertising, and other forms of content marketing. Therefore, mobile is really a delivery platform like the desktop computer, except it is always with the customer.

Using responsive web design, we can deliver a customer experience that is tailored to the specific device, or platform, upon which the customer is engaging with us. Responsive web design might mean delivering a mobile experience tailored to a specific platform, that is, Android smartphone. Responsive web design can also include responses that are personal to the particular customer if they are logged in or as a result of their search query keywords.

Applications on mobile devices (known as "apps") and especially free apps have exploded and provide an advertising opportunity. However, because of the difficulties of the many different types of ad browsers and delivering ads within the application, mobile ads have not been as targeted as traditional advertisements and were slow to develop.[15] Now, there is more opportunity to advertise on mobile applications with improvements in in-app advertising formats and delivery platforms.

Mobile Advertising

Mobile interactions have exploded, with the majority of e-mails now being opened on mobile devices. In fact, video advertising and visual images as well as gaming are good applications for the mobile platform as smartphones and mobile devices become faster. Global ad spend is growing at double-digit rates and will increase to nearly $515 billion in 2023, growing more quickly than spending on newspapers or radio by far.[16]

---

[15]Aquino. 2013. "No Mobile Cookies? Criteo Defiantly Rolls Out Mobile Web Tracking Solution." https://www.adexchanger.com/mobile/no-mobile-cookies-criteo-defiantly-rolls-out-mobile-web-tracking-solution/.

[16]Fisher. 2019. "US Programmatic Ad Spending Forecast 2019." https://www.emarketer.com/content/us-programmatic-ad-spending-forecast-2019, (accessed January 9, 2020).

However, advertising spending has been disproportionate. Spending on mobile advertising in 2014 was about 10 percent of ad spend, in spite of the fact that Americans spent more than 10 percent of their time on their mobile devices.[17] There was a disconnect in spending versus time spent as marketers adjusted to the new world of digital convergence.

In fact, Americans now spend almost 20 percent of their time on mobile devices.[18] Mobile advertising in 2020 is predicted to be 43 percent of all media ad spend, more than all other traditional media channels combined. Advertisers have caught up to market trends and are placing their ads where their customers are on an hourly basis.[19]

Digital Advertising Landscape

It is not surprising that we encountered this problem of the disconnect between user time spent and amount spent on advertising as the digital advertising landscape in general is fast-moving and changing daily. Digital advertising has expanded rapidly over the last few years and advertisers have had to struggle to keep up-to-date. As stated previously, the initial idea upon seeing a web browser on a screen was for advertisers and their agencies to view Internet advertising as a small form of television advertising. These ad formats are known as banner ads. Click-through rates were initially high until users became used to the ads and did not seek value.

Today's advertisements that are successful are visual, interactive, and often include a video format. The Internet Advertising Bureau has a series of formats that are considered "rising stars" that include rich media formats. These ads typically have higher engagement rates, sometimes two or

---

[17]Perlberg. 2014. "Mobile-Ad Spending Leaps, but Trails User Growth," *Wall Street Journal.* http://www.wsj.com/articles/mobile-ad-spending-leaps-but-trails-user-growth-1405969018, (accessed August 12, 2019).

[18]He. 2019. "Average US Time Spent with Mobile in 2019 Has Increased." https://www.emarketer.com/content/average-us-time-spent-with-mobile-in-2019-has-increased, (accessed January 9, 2020).

[19]eMarketer. 2018. "Mobile Ad Spending to Surpass All Traditional Media Combined by 2020." https://www.emarketer.com/content/mobile-ad-spending-to-surpass-all-traditional-media-combined-by-2020, (accessed January 9, 2020).

three times higher than traditional banner ads.[20] Much of these rich format ads are video advertisements, with an estimate that over 25 percent of digital advertising is video.

Advertising today has become more complex than in the early days of the Internet. Terrence Kawaja and his associates at Luma Partners have created a series of graphics that attempt to explain the complexity, but these charts can also be daunting.[21] Delivering advertising online has depended heavily on cookies (code that let website owners and advertisers know when someone has previously visited a site) and on developing an in-depth understanding of the customer by integrating data from data suppliers such as Experian, Epsilon, and Acxiom. The goal is to try to identify the customer, if not by name, as closely as possible. If you ever noticed that you looked for an item, did not buy it, and then found it on an advertisement on your web browser, that is because of using cookies and a practice known as retargeting. Ads can also be delivered based on the context of the consumer's search patterns or e-mail communications, their online behavior (identified if logged in or unidentified if not), or their geographical location.

Advertisers will have to become more creative with the use of cookies as third-party cookies are under attack. Google announced that third-party cookies will be phased out by 2020.[22] Firefox is moving in that direction as well. Apple's Safari browser will now have Intelligent Tracking Prevention to stop third parties from tracking users as they browse from site to site after a 24 hour period.[23] These changes mean that advertisers will have to be more creative in their targeting efforts, such as an increased use of location data to serve advertisements.

---

[20]eMarketer. 2014. "IAB Rising Stars Ads Outperform Standard Banners," *Article*. http://www.emarketer.com/Article/IAB-Rising-Stars-Ads-Outperform-Standard-Banners/1010761, (accessed October 13, 2019).

[21]T. Kawaja. 2010. "DISPLAY LUMAscape," *Slideshare*. https://www.slideshare.net/tkawaja/luma-display-ad-tech-landscape-2010-1231, (accessed January 9, 2020).

[22]G. Sterling. January 14, 2020. "Google Chrome: Third-party cookies will be gone by 2020." https://marketingland.com/google-chrome-third-party-cookies-will-be-gone-by-2022-274313, (accessed January 20, 2020).

[23]G. Marvin. June 7, 2017. "How Apple's Intelligent Tracking Prevention works and why Google and Facebook could benefit the most." https://marketingland.com/apple-safari-intelligent-ad-tracking-what-we-know-216865, (accessed January 20, 2020).

Basically, online advertising evolved from using simple ad exchanges to place ads to a complicated system of "real-time bidding" (RTB) whereby the majority of ads are delivered automatically through ad networks. These ads are then shown automatically via social media networks such as Twitter and Facebook, ad servers such as Double Click (now Google Marketing Platforms) and other publisher tools. Advertisers either pay per "click" or per "impression" for the ad and conversion rates are typically low. In addition, most of the online display advertising continues to be concentrated among the top firms. For example, Google (YouTube) and Facebook attract almost 70 percent of advertising revenue and are becoming known as the "duopoly." This concentration makes it difficult to launch a new business and fund it through advertising.[24] However, the surge in product searches on Amazon and the wealth of customer information it possesses for ad targeting makes it a strong candidate to take advertising dollars away from Google and Facebook in the coming years. The concentrated ad market and the complicated business of RTB and programmatic or "automatic" ad buying have both transformed media buying and will continue to do so. Advertising online today is increasingly "programmatic" or controlled by advertising placement networks and not by individual media-placement decisions. By 2021, it is estimated that 88 percent of digital display advertising will be transacted programmatically.[25]

Advertisements will continue to be placed on mobile devices, social media, and anywhere else the consumer is likely to be. However, it is likely that conversion rates will continue to be lower than those of other types of media such as e-mail and paid search. Advertising is still best used for brand-building, even in digital marketing. In fact, 37.7 percent of those who interacted with a mobile rising stars ad (new, improved ad formats) said the experience improved brand impression, compared to

[24]Poggi. 2019. "Google-Facebook duopoly set to lose some of its share of ad spend." https://adage.com/article/digital/duopoly-loses-share-ad-spend/316692, (accessed January 9, 2020).

[25]Fisher. 2019. "US Programmatic Ad Spending Forecast 2019." https://www.emarketer.com/content/us-programmatic-ad-spending-forecast-2019, (accessed January 8, 2020).

20.6 percent for standard mobile banner ads. The benefits of social media and other marketing channels discussed in this book cannot be overlooked and should be seen as supplementing any digital advertising plan.[26]

What to Do Next after Chapter 6

1. Imagine you are creating a content marketing campaign for your own or another company product or service. Relating back to Chapter 2, what is your unique positioning and how will you create value for your customers?

2. Based on your target customer, select three social platforms that you think will be most likely to reach that target customer.

3. Design a content marketing plan for that product or service using the example in Figure 6.4. Can you use one piece of content and "repurpose" it across multiple social platforms?

Discussion Questions

Discussion 6.1: Why do you think some managers are resistant to the idea of engaging in SMM? What could you do or say to convince your reluctant boss that SMM could be a good idea in a specific business setting?

Discussion 6.2: Imagine that recently your company has been trying to convert participants on its various social media platforms to customers. What advice can you give those in charge about increasing conversion?

Discussion 6.3: Among paid, owed, earned, and shared media, which is the most credible to customers on social media and why? Give an example from your own or others' experiences.

Discussion 6.4: Explain the concept of CE. What is its relevance to digital marketing? Contrast that with the role of CE in the offline retailing environment. Are they the same?

---

[26]Perlberg. 2014. "Mobile Ads Breach Historic Barrier," *Wall Street Journal*. B1.

Glossary

Content marketing: Using the creation of meaningful content around the brand for marketing purposes to foster engagement and brand loyalty.

Customer engagement: How involved customers are with the brand as well as a process for keeping them involved.

Paid, earned, owned, and shared media: Different categories of media, with examples of paid being advertising, earned being word of mouth, owned being a company's own asset, and shared being something co-created with the customer.

Social media marketing (SMM): Using forms of social media for brand and product promotion and to foster engagement.

Social media monitoring: Keeping track of social media activity, often through a commercial application.

Social media networking sites: Sites through which users share content and comments with each other. The major sites are highly sought after as advertising platforms.

Storytelling: Using customer stories and case studies to help customers better relate to and remember your brand.

PART III

Context

CHAPTER 7

Customer Relationship Management (CRM) and the Role of Leadership in Digital Marketing

Marketing Management versus Customer Relationship Marketing

All the changes in technologies for marketing discussed so far have substantially altered the role of the customer in the marketing process and the relationship between the customer and the marketer. These final chapters discuss the context for that change and focus on activities where the marketer can still affect what happens in this relationship. Creating a sound database, developing strong leadership, and being aware of the complex legal environment are all part of the task of marketing.

This book is called *Digital Marketing Management* to indicate the shift in marketing toward the use of marketing management technologies which facilitate engagement of the customer and personalization of each customer's particular experience with the firm. If customers interact with firms today through digital technology, then these interactions must change the process of how managers think about their customers and manage the entire process of marketing of the firm. Chapters 7 through 9 are dedicated to exploring techniques to manage the customer relationship across channels and to organize such activities within the firm.

It is important to remember that the core of competitive advantage is having a product or service that customers wish to purchase at the price the firm is offering. Competitive advantage is not necessarily dependent upon digital marketing methods. Digital channels can enhance and complement the firm's existing channels but are not a substitute for that which sustains growth in the firm.[1]

We have looked at the learning organization to understand how firms can use digital technology to learn in Chapter 2. Learning comes from internal resources, the competitive environment, our customers, and suppliers/partners. Learning is facilitated by, but not limited to, the use of digital technology, which by its nature supports the learning process. There are two types of market sensing capabilities, those from the firm to the outside world and those from the outside world to the firm. It is useful therefore to think of digital technology as playing a pivotal but supporting role in facilitating the learning processes of the organization.

There are many ways digital technologies can be crucial in learning processes. Crowdsourcing technologies can help us understand customer needs, for example, and private label social media networks can help us interact with our suppliers. Data from learning processes flows from the outside into the firm and from the inside out, forming a continuous feedback loop whereby the firm continuously updates and creates itself. In fact, the concept of market orientation itself means that the firm is constantly processing information about the marketplace to meet customer needs and expectations.

Although there are some companies that rely primarily on Internet technology for their business models, in the Fortune 500, many of the largest firms produce a product or service that is more reliant on the physical world of stores, distribution arms, and factories. Most firms use many marketing channels of both distribution and communication. Facebook is still only a fraction of the size of Walmart, the leader in the Fortune 500 and other firms such as Amazon.com have yet to reach other than marginal profitability.[2]

Therefore, every firm can benefit from advances in digital technology and digital marketing. Without the emphasis on one-way communication

---

[1]E. Penrose. 1959. *The Theory of the Growth of the Firm* (New York, NY: John Wiley & Sons).

[2]Slate. 2014. "With Wall Street's Support, Jeff Bezos Can Conquer the World Without Earning a Profit," *Article*. https://slate.com/business/2014/01/amazon-earnings-how-jeff-bezos-gets-investors-to-believe-in-him.html, (accessed October 13, 2019).

and focusing on conversation in marketing, the process becomes one of slowly developing the relationship with the customer instead of seeking a one-time transaction. We have moved from a product focus to a customer focus, from transactions to relationships, from acquisition to retention, from product profitability to customer profitability, and from trial and error to testing and measurement.

However, marketing management thought principles as they are usually taught have not changed from the 1950s. The traditional process of marketing management is said to include the principles of product, price, promotion, and place. The manager is like an orchestra conductor or puppeteer, adjusting these elements of what is known as the marketing "mix." As the manager makes these changes, the customers, like an orchestra, respond to commands. Lower the price, alter the product slightly, or put out a promotional coupon, and the consumer buys more.

In the new world of marketing thought, consumers *do* respond to what are known as marketing actions, but the process has become more complex and individualized. Customers interact with the firm and each other and often initiate the conversation. So rather than marketing being an orchestrated process with the marketer as conductor, the process of marketing today is more like music made by a jazz ensemble, where the players work off of each other to create a work of music. This new way of imagining marketing requires new processes to be managed and measured.

Marketers not only have the capability to personalize and customize communications but to interact with individual consumers in ways not imagined previously. Using digital technology, marketers can rapidly seek out the most influential consumers—those known as thought leaders—and engage them in such a way as to influence their thinking and writing about a product. Marketers can interact on social media with specific customers to answer their questions individually and communicate with them directly. There has been a shift in emphasis from managing a process of marketing tasks to campaigns that are integrated across channels and seek to engage the customer across these multiple channels.

Marketers want to engage the customer but also struggle for a way to measure the success of these interactions or engagements. The traditional way of analyzing customer response to advertising was attention, interest, desire, and action (AIDA). Although AIDA focuses on how to move the customer through a process, in the digital age, we focus on treating different customers differently in a process often called customer relationship management (CRM; see Chapter 3). Sometimes this process is called customer relationship marketing because relationships are difficult to manage in order to get the desired result; customer relationship marketing as a term focuses on the customer more and the process less. CRM can be defined as the "process of managing and measuring customer interactions across various channels with the goal of optimizing the value of the customer relationship to both parties to the exchange process." Often this process involves building a customer profile or profiles—the characteristics of different customer segments that allow us to select different treatments for different groups. CRM technology can be powerful, as using personalized communications based on customer profiles can significantly improve the results of marketing programs. As an alternative to identify, differentiate, interact, and customize (IDIC), Martha Rogers and Don Peppers suggest the IDIC profile,[3] indicating that each customer should receive unique communications, offers, and interactions. In our research, we suggest that we personalize communications and customize product offerings, which means that IDIC becomes IDICP—identify, differentiate, interact, and customize/personalize. Increasingly CRM focuses on using information to improve the overall customer experience.

Creating a seamless customer experience across products and channels usually requires the tools of CRM systems because these tools allow companies to manage their customer interactions and measure them to determine which approaches are most effective for a specific customer or set of customers. These systems have long been advocated in marketing literature, in both practitioner and academic studies. However, there are problems with implementation and these systems are really only effective if supported through the corporation. Another problem with these systems is the proliferation of marketing communications tools that we talked about earlier in this text as well. Multichannel marketing has made CRM much more difficult.

---

[3] Peppers and Rogers Group. 2014. "Telecommunications Capabilities," *PDF*. http://www.peppersandrogersgroup.com/DocumentDownload.aspx?Doc_ID=31637, (accessed October 13, 2019).

CRM tools vary from contact management systems like salesforce.com to more complex implementation systems for larger companies like Eloqua or SAP. We can also include in the CRM category marketing automation tools like Marketo™. Although these tools are often campaign-based, they are also used to retain customers and enhance their overall experience with the firm. All these tools are designed to track and manage customer information, automate customer interactions, simplify workflow, and monitor and track results. The idea used to be to get a "360-degree" view of the customer and all interactions, although I would argue that the relationships are now more complex and difficult to chart.

The need for this type of system has occurred because of the trends documented in the previous section of this book. Not only can we engage more with the customer but we can do so across many marketing channels. In order to manage this process effectively there has to be a shift from the internal processes of the firm to the external processes of the customer. This shift is known as "customer experience marketing" (CEM) and requires a services marketing orientation. This trend means that marketers must consider how the consumer interacts with the product/brand and must do so across all available channels. The customer has come to expect that the marketer will engage with him across all channels consistently, including understanding past purchases and interactions.

In fact, the foundation of CRM interactions is building trust with the customer. Salesforce.com has found that customers that trust the company are more likely to be loyal, recommend the company, buy products and services in greater quantity and more frequently, spend more money with the company, and share their experiences.[4] Companies like Wells Fargo, Bespoke and Activision all use CRM systems to their advantage in managing customer relationships and building trust.

---

[4]Salesforce. n.d. "4 Examples of Businesses Using CRM to Improve Productivity and Efficiency." https://www.salesforce.com/crm/examples/?gclid=CjwKCAiApOvw BRBUEiwAcZGdGEuPv4GBipCV_AhxbvPeoZU-gJCFWwIXa11h1IKLucWSfcz1 DfJ7wxoCJ00QAvD_BwE&d=70130000000liRf&DCMP=KNC-Google&ef_id= CjwKCAiApOvwBRBUEiwAcZGdGEuPv4GBipCV_AhxbvPeoZU-gJCFWwIXa 11h1IKLucWSfcz1DfJ7wxoCJ00QAvD_BwE:G:s&s_kwcid=AL!4604!3!98661552 059!b!!g!!+magic+quadrant+crm&gclsrc=aw.ds#, (accessed January 12, 2020).

Multichannel (Omni-Channel Reality): "Always on Marketing"

As discussed in Chapter 1, the developments in Internet technology which resulted in digital marketing mean that the process of marketing is an interactive, conversational one that in the customer's mind occurs 24/7. This trend of a marketing engagement model that never rests is called "always on" marketing. So, if a customer buys something online, writes about it in social media, and returns it in the store, the customer expects the marketer to have knowledge of these prior transactions and to understand what has happened and respond accordingly. Especially in consumer markets but also in business-to-business markets, this type of response could not be possible without the applications and their under- lying data facilitated by digital technology. Increasingly, CRM systems are focusing on "real-time" responses and analysis[5] such as "real-time" adver- tising. Multichannel marketing has become omni-channel marketing, which means customers expect the same relationship across all channels 24 hours a day. CRM and marketing automation increasingly help firms to achieve this objective and meet customer expectations. In fact, Gartner predicts that by 2022, 70 percent of customer interactions will involve such as machine learning applications, chatbots, and mobile messaging, up from 15 percent in 2018.[6]

One of the challenges of multichannel marketing in terms of CRM is measurement. The reason measurement is a challenge is because the mul- tichannel experiences occur across a variety of dimensions. Technology can certainly facilitate the multichannel customer interface and help reap substantial benefits and offers the best hope for being able to manage and measure this difficult process. In fact, customer service organizations who incorporate artificial intelligence in their multichannel communications have the opportunity to increase operational efficiency by 25 percent.

It is difficult to capture in just a simple chart or matrix everything that is going on in the multichannel process. In Figure 7.1 I have adapted

---

[5]Saba. 2017. "How Real-Time Analytics are Reshaping Marketing," *CallRail.* https:// www.callrail.com/blog/real-time-analytics-marketing/, (accessed October 13, 2019).
[6]Gartner Magic Quadrant for the CRM Customer Engagement Center, Report pub- lished June 11, 2019.

the traditional House of Quality[7] for new product development to the House of Quality for multichannel marketing. The House of Quality was developed as a methodology to ensure that all relevant dimensions were included in the development of a new product, user needs, competitor competencies, and our own internal capabilities. Similarly, we need to think about all of these dimensions together.

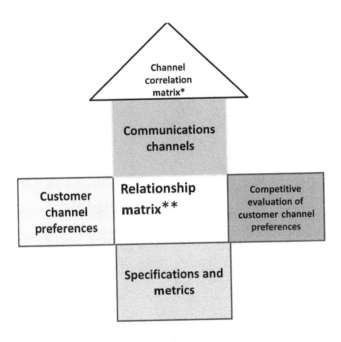

*How customer channels work together
**Customer channel preferences, our channels

Figure 7.1 The House of Quality for multichannel and digital marketing

Using the House of Quality analogy, we must consider the customer channel preference, our current capabilities, and competitive capabilities in developing our multichannel strategy and measurements. For example, the customer base has a certain communication channel preference. The

---

[7]G. Urban and J. Hauser. 1993. *Design and Marketing of New Products.* 2nd ed. (Massachusetts, MA: MIT).

first question to ask is are we spending our money where our customers are spending their time? If the customer is primarily focused on mobile devices and we communicate rarely over that channel, then there is a mismatch of resources that the analysis will highlight. The overlap in customer channel preferences and our strategy in Figure 7.2 represents an opportunity to develop our communications in those preferred channels. So, the first step to developing multichannel metrics is to develop a strategy that is consistent with customer preferences. Only by understanding first where the customer is spending time and second, how they like to communicate, can we hope to develop an effective multichannel measurement program.[8]

Figure 7.2 *Customer channel preference versus our channel strategy*

For example, we know that for many years customers spent more time online but advertising budgets were still focused on traditional media.[9] Another example of channel "mismatch" is the tablet market. Tablets are rapidly outperforming mobile devices for shopping. The screen sizes are larger and allow for easier shopping. Not surprisingly, average order

---

[8]D. Zahay. 2014. "How to Take Charge of Multichannel Metrics," *Digital Marketing and Analytics blog.* http://digitalmktganalytics.blogspot.com/2014/02/how-to-take-charge-of-multichannel.html, (accessed October 13, 2019).

[9]eMarketer. 2014. "Despite Time Spent Mobile Still Lacks Ad Spend in the U.S," *Article.* http://www.emarketer.com/Article/Despite-Time-Spent-Mobile-Still-Lacks-Ad-Spend-US/1010788, (accessed October 13, 2019).

values, retail traffic, and conversion rates are higher on tablets.[10] Yet again, the spending on tablets lagged the activity on the tablet by the consumer. The relationship matrix takes an honest look at our channels versus those preferred by the customer to ensure that there is a match (Figure 7.2). If the customer is primarily focused on mobile devices and we communicate rarely over that channel, then there is a mismatch of resources that the relationship matrix will highlight.

We also need to develop a matrix of how our channels are meant to work together, known as a channel correlation matrix. Do we create a blog post, send out the information by e-mail, and then drive customers to our website? How do we perceive that channels will work together to create customer engagement? We also need to look at our competitors and see how they are focused in terms of customer channels. Is there a better mix between their channel choices and ours in terms of where the customers spend their time?

Finally, in Specifications and Metrics, we determine which channels we will use, how frequently, and how we will measure the effectiveness of our multichannel communications. For example, we know there is a clear disconnect between the time spent on mobile devices and ad spend. This trend is only going to be more prominent as users have been flocking to mobile devices in greater and greater numbers. Our matrices would show the time spent on the channel by the consumer, cross-device and cross-channel synergies, the corresponding resources we have allocated to that channel, and highlight how we can best measure results. CRM systems, in particular, must now manage results across mobile and social channels.

Measurement and Management

Once the program is put together, the process of measuring the results of CRM initiatives can be tricky. Instead of looking at the results of a single campaign, we must try to explain results across channels, called channel

---

[10]Adler. 2013. "Tablets Are Becoming More Important than Smartphones for Online Shopping, But Retailers Aren't Ready," *Business Insider.* https://www.businessinsider .com/tablet-shoppers-in-mobile-commerce-2013-11, (accessed October 13, 2019).

attribution. In a customer-oriented measurement world, we use terms such as "share of wallet" (the percentage of a customer's spending on a particular product line that we have) rather than "market share."

Therefore, the core of any CRM system is its data management system (Chapter 9). The three foundations of CRM are often said to be data maintenance, marketing, and follow-on customer service. Together, these internal disciplines allow us to engage the customer and measure the results. Data drives every step of the CRM process. Tesco is a UK-based grocer that began a loyalty program in 1995. Quite often the best reason to start a customer loyalty program is to collect data on the customer, which the company did. Gradually, the company built a behavioral database and began segmentation and targeting using that data and created offers, promotions, and communications specific to each customer. The program yielded strong successes for the retailer; although recent trends in grocery retailing such as multichannel shopping (particularly online) and the tendency for shopping in more than one store have challenged Tesco, overall, the program has been a success[11,12]

In spite of the benefits of CRM systems, half or more fail to meet their ROI (return on investment) targets. It seems as though half of the companies are building a system and half are abandoning the system. The reasons for abandonment and failure are often more organizational than technological. For example, of the eight Gartner Group CRM building blocks,[13] for example, most of them are not technology-based but rather leadership-focused.

Most of the factors that influence the success and failure of digital outcomes are also managerial. Senior management buy-in, leadership, and

---

[11]Ruddick. 2014. "Clubcard Built the Tesco of Today, But It Could Be Time to Ditch It." http://www.telegraph.co.uk/finance/newsbysector/retailandconsumer/10577685/Clubcard-built-the-Tesco-of-today-but-it-could-be-time-to-ditch-it.html, (accessed October 13, 2019).

[12]Fleming. 2019. "How Tesco revolutionised loyalty with Clubcard: The Inside Story." https://www.marketingweek.com/tesco-clubcard-loyalty/, (accessed January 12, 2020).

[13]Gartner. 2001. "Eight Building Blocks of CRM: A Framework for Success," PDF. https://www.academia.edu/2178648/Eight_building_blocks_of_CRM_A_framework_for_success, (accessed January 12, 2020).

alignment of goals all facilitate digital outcomes. McKinsey & Company asked 850 C-level executives about digital engagement of customers, big data, and digital engagement of employees, automation, and digital innovation of products. The biggest challenges were managerial and structural, such as internal organization and good quality data.

The Importance of Data Quality in Measurement

In fact, the Corporate Executive Board (CEB) Marketing Leadership Council[14] echoes that B2B marketers in particular are struggling with implementing data analytics and measurement solutions in their firms. Not surprisingly, the issue is often one of data quality. Poor data quality and analytics capability leads to a lack of meaningful insight, which in turn can lead to a lack of funding for data quality and analytics efforts.

The result of poor data quality is a vicious circle where marketers cannot get the proper funding for their efforts. Our research results reinforce this idea but also link data quality to customer performance. In our recent paper in the *Journal of Interactive Marketing* that was voted best paper of 2014, coauthors James Peltier, Don Lehman, and I present a model with empirical evidence of this relationship from the financial industry, both B2B and B2C applications.[15]

Vicious Circle of Data Quality

In the article mentioned above we measure customer data quality in the organizational context. We not only show the linkages from customer data quality to ultimate firm performance as measured by growth, we explore this result in the context of the firm's organizational and management structure. Without a culture that values analytics and data, data

---

[14]CEB Marketing Leadership Council. 2014. "The Digital Evolution in B2B Marketing," *Web Article*. https://www.cebglobal.com/content/dam/cebglobal/us/EN/best-practices-decision-support/marketing-communications/pdfs/CEB-Mktg-B2B-Digital-Evolution.pdf, (accessed January 12, 2020).

[15]J. W. Peltier, D. Zahay, and D. R. Lehmann. 2013. "Organizational Learning and CRM Success: A Model for Linking Organizational Practices, Customer Data Quality and Performance," *Journal of Interactive Marketing* 27, pp. 1-13.

quality cannot result. Culture means not only top management support, but parts of the organization working together.

Therefore, the top three reasons I see why organizations cannot achieve analytics success necessary for a successful CRM program are as follows:

1. Lack of a cooperative culture that supports data quality.
2. Lack of support by upper management for data quality efforts.
3. The resulting poor-quality data that leads to poor decisions.

These relationships are indicated in Figure 7.3. The executive leads by creating a culture that fosters cross-functional cooperation and the integration of efforts between marketing and IT. These organizational factors then lead to better data sharing and data quality, customer performance (share of wallet, retention, lifetime customer value), and ultimately firm performance (growth in sales and profits). The key role of the chief executive includes all aspects of CRM implementation, including the customer experience (CX).[16]

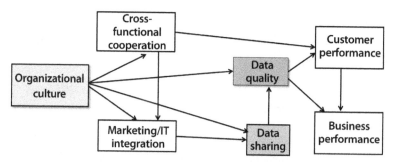

Figure 7.3 The key role of the top executive in data quality

The Importance of Middle Management

If data quality gets lost in the shuffle in CRM implementation, so also does the role of middle management. Despite the promise of data management and big data, many of the firms investing in customer information

---

[16]Sporton. 2020. "It's All About Trust: The Importance of CX in 2020." https://tdwi.org/articles/2020/01/06/bi-all-importance-of-cx-in-2020.aspx, (accessed January 12, 2020).

technology have witnessed limited financial success from their data-driven efforts designed to get close to customers.

As a consequence, many adopters became disillusioned and learn for themselves that customer-centricity is difficult to accomplish, requires a high level of coordination between IT and marketing, and involves a cultural shift with regard to how customer data are integrated and shared within and between functional areas.[17]

The interpersonal and organizational factors of big data implementation, which my coauthors and I have been studying since 2007, have only recently come to the forefront as critical to the success of CRM projects. In fact, our research shows that in companies where middle management believes it is involved in customer data management and feels supported, data quality improves and so does firm performance. So, it is critical to involve middle management in customer information processes.

Middle managers often take a back seat or are assigned limited importance in organizations. However, these managers play a key role in strategy execution, particularly in cross-functional efforts such as CRM and Big Data. As indicated above, work from the Gartner Group suggests that among the building blocks of successful CRM implementation, which is a customer data-dependent application, are organizational collaboration and organizational processes. Also, as the millennial generation becomes more influential in purchasing decisions and moves into middle management roles, their style of decision making must be taken into account.

What does it mean to involve middle management and improve organizational collaboration? These reported results are based on 128 survey responses from managers in the financial services industry. In our survey we asked middle managers three key questions to which they responded on a scale of 1 to 5, with 5 being strongly agree and 1 being strongly disagree. The questions were as follows:

1. We feel comfortable calling our upper management when the need arises.

---

[17]D.L. Zahay and J. Peltier. 2008. "Interactive Strategy Formation: Organizational and Entrepreneurial Factors Related to Effective Customer Information Systems Practices in B2B Firms," *Industrial Marketing Management* 37, no. 2, pp. 191-205.

2. Our marketing management is responsive to our customer information ideas.

3. Marketing managers can easily schedule meetings with upper management.

In these data, marketing management support was strongly correlated with customer data quality, which in another research study mentioned above we have demonstrated to be related to ultimate firm performance. In a regression analysis, marketing manager support was also significant in predicting customer data quality. These results are consistent with other research we have conducted and show the importance of involving middle management in the process. It appears that in order to ensure data quality, the firm's middle management and upper management must have an open and communicative relationship. Consistent with findings from practice, the most successful organizational relationships in these companies had a clear role for middle management in translating the language of quality customer information management to upper management. These results are also consistent with several schools of thought in strategy, which support the idea that strategy comes from the bottom up, or at least from middle management back to top management.

Therefore, CRM implementations are complex and rely on top management support and good quality data to be successful. The tenets of organizing for customer data quality are shown in Figure 7.4. An agreed, shared vision and proper reward structures can go a long way in creating good customer data quality by getting the organization to work together. While the stakes are high, the rewards can be great for successful companies. Every year, The Media company (TMC) announces their CRM Excellence Award winners and highlights the companies in its magazine, *CUSTOMER*.[18] The companies in these cases exemplify improving the customer experience by improving the flow of information needed to retain customers.

---

[18]CUSTOMER Magazine Announces Winners of the 2019 CRM Excellence Award. 2019. https://www.customerzone360.com/topics/customer/articles/442475-customer-magazine-announces-winners-the-2019-crm-excellence.htm, (accessed January 12, 2020).

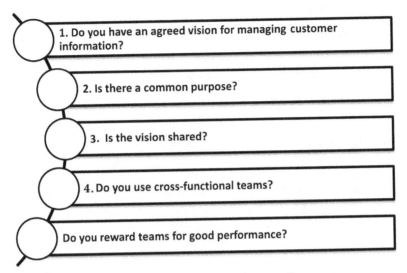

1. Do you have an agreed vision for managing customer information?

2. Is there a common purpose?

3. Is the vision shared?

4. Do you use cross-functional teams?

Do you reward teams for good performance?

Figure 7.4 How to organize for customer data quality

What to Do Next after Chapter 7

1. Think about your own company or a company you might choose and perform a quality analysis for digital marketing. Is the company communicating where its customers are? What about versus competitors? Do the communications channels work together and which are most effective (Figures 7.1 and 7.2)?

2. Based on your analysis in question 1, develop recommendations for the company to align its channel strategy more closely with customer needs.

3. Analyze your own company or another firm in terms of Figure 7.3; is your organization optimized for customer data quality? If not, what needs to be done to get there?

Discussion Questions

Discussion 7.1: Think about organizational issues and data issues and the impact on delivery of exceptional customer service. Have you encountered any customer service instances in which people in the same organization seemed to be giving you different information or advice? Why do you think this happened?

Discussion 7.2: Select one of the four examples of a successful CRM implementations in this link provided by salesforce (https://www.salesforce.com/crm/examples/). Briefly describe what made that firm successful. How do you think these techniques can be applied to your organization?

Discussion 7.3: For the company you selected above, relate the course material to the company selected. How did the company achieve CRM success using any or all of the suggested techniques in the readings? Was there anything else they did that was not mentioned?

Discussion 7.4: What would your first three steps be if you were assigned to spearhead a CRM implementation in your company and why?

Glossary

360-degree view: Being able to integrate data across the company to understand past and current purchase behaviors, web activities, and the like; requires integrating data "silos."

Always on marketing: Being able to respond to the customers 24/7.

Channel correlation matrix: Using a matrix to determine how channels work together to achieve goals.

CRM: An acronym for customer relationship management, an attempt to provide meaningful interactions with the customer.

Customer experience: The customer's interactions with a company or brand over time.

Omni-channel marketing: Marketing across channels in a seamless way; sometimes referred to as being channel "agnostic."

Relationship matrix: A matrix of our channels versus those preferred by the customer to ensure that there is a match.

CHAPTER 8

Legal Issues: Data Privacy, Security, and Intellectual Property

The Right to Privacy?

In the United States, we have no expressly stated right to privacy. Scour the United States Constitution's Bill of Rights and you will see privacy is not expressly mentioned. Some case law has established right to privacy, most notably *Roe v. Wade* (1973), but so far, a provision for true data privacy has not been mentioned. The reason for this lack of attention is based on the historical foundations of the United States itself.

Calvin Coolidge said, "the business of America is business." To prosper, business needs data. So, although freedom of religion and separation of church and state were important founding principles in the United States, also important was the freedom of commerce. The Revolution, after all, started in part over perceived unfair taxation of tea imported into the country. The eighteenth century was also the age of *laissez-faire* capitalism as articulated by Adam Smith. The idea of free trade and free markets was allowed to flourish in the newly founded United States. As we discussed in Chapter 1, data must flow along the value chain to help create value for the customer and profits for the firm. Customer information is included in that data.

For many years, data flowed freely in this country to facilitate commerce. A key element of this free flow of commerce was based on the trust that the consumer had that the data would be used in a responsible manner. However, let's face it: things moved more slowly in the eighteenth century. As noted in Chapter 1, there have been trends in the last

20 years that have fueled e-commerce and digital marketing growth. The growth of the Internet and the ability to manage large-scale databases in a real-time fashion has meant that marketers have the ability to know more about us than we really might want them to know and to track our behavior online using a variety of mechanisms.

Earlier, in the context of online advertising, we talked about tracking cookies that are placed on our computers by various websites and search engines. These cookies can help by remembering our preferences when we return to a website or by delivering a targeted advertisement. On the other hand, if we don't want the enhanced web experience, we can delete cookies or use ad blocking software on our browser. It's rather like direct mail in concept. If we did not have data management companies cleansing data and helping firms target us, we would receive far more direct mail solicitations than we receive today and they would be of less interest to us. Similarly, if we decide not to enable cookies, we have a generic browsing experience full of ads for refinancing our mortgage and reducing troublesome "belly fat!"

Consumer Attitudes toward Privacy

Nonetheless, data privacy is an emotionally charged issue. First, consumers often confuse data privacy and data security, which will be discussed later. Emotions run high not only about data security breaches, but consumers also have negative attitudes toward marketing and a fear of the government having too much information about individuals and using it in an intrusive way. When speaking about data privacy we refer to personally identifiable information (PII). Dr. Alan Westin, who before his death was a professor of law at Columbia University, did a lot of research on public attitudes toward privacy and found that most of us were willing to trade privacy for something of value. Consumers in general want more control over their PII but aren't sure they want to go through all the steps necessary to control information. Would you really want to tell every website you interact with how to handle your information?

A good exercise is to look at the privacy policy of a large company like Amazon.com. Amazon's privacy policy may be found in the link in this footnote.[1] You will see that the policy does not say that the company will not resell your information. It does say what the company will do with the information in a forthright manner and is one of the best examples of a privacy policy. Many companies that have gotten into trouble over PII have not followed their privacy policies; so if the policy is in place, it should be followed.

Nonetheless, in various studies the majority of individuals feel uncomfortable with activities such as behavioral targeting of advertising, with generational differences seen. Younger consumers are more likely to feel comfortable with how data is used today to target advertising to them across various devices. There have been a number of surveys recently on data privacy, with some indicating that consumers think brands are benefitting more from data sharing than the customer sharing the data.[2] So the climate is now set for consumers to be open to stricter data privacy laws in the United States.

The EU Approach

In contrast, the European Union has always viewed data privacy differently. The 1995[3] EU directive allows the data "subject" right of access to data and the right to find out about the processing of data. The European Union, while understanding that data is important to the flow of commerce, considers that data about the customer belongs to the customer and not to the company or entity processing the data.

With such differing standards, how do companies do business with the European Union? For many years in the United States, companies who complied with what were known as the Safe Harbor practices were allowed to do business with companies and consumers in EU countries.

---

[1]Amazon. 2014. "Amazon.com Privacy Notice," *Website*. https://www.amazon.com/gp/help/customer/display.html?nodeId=468496, (accessed October 13, 2019).

[2]Factual Inc. 2019. "Consumers & Data Privacy Perceptions," *PDF*. https://s3.amazonaws.com/factual-content/marketing/downloads/Factual-Consumers-Data-Privacy-Perceptions-Report.pdf, (accessed January 14, 2020).

[3]European Parliament and Council. 2014. "Protection of Personal Data," *European Parliament and Council Directive*. http://eur-lex.europa.eu/legal-content/EN/TXT/HTML/?uri=URISERV:l14012&from=en&isLegissum=true, (accessed October 13, 2019).

These provisions are listed as the following: notice, choice, onward transfer, access, security, data integrity, and enforcement.[4]

The Federal Trade Commission (FTC) has suggested Fair Information Practices principles which include remarkably similar categories to those of the EU in terms of notice/awareness, choice/consent, access/participation, and enforcement/redress. Unfortunately, these practices are still guidelines. The FTC in its guidelines on this issue has suggested that companies design privacy into their products and services, simplify choices, and provide greater transparency for data, but so far these suggestions do not have the weight of federal legislation.

In part because of the lack of federal data privacy legislation in the United States, the EU wanted stronger enforcement of its privacy policy and adopted the General Data Protection Rules (GDPR) in 2016 and they were generally implemented in 2018. These rules require strict processes for processing data and for obtaining consent and do not apply only to companies doing business physically in Europe. Companies transferring data to the United States are affected as well as those conducting business on the Internet.[5] In short, just about every business is affected by the GDPR.

In addition, the GDPR includes a right to be forgotten, which will allow entities to essentially "opt out" of being found by search engines like Google.[6] Under certain circumstances, a consumer might ask for personal data to be removed from a company's records. You may have noticed that websites often notify you these days that they are obtaining your consent to use cookies. This type of procedure is an attempt to enforce the GDPR rules. More information can be found in the excellent blog post by the late Dr. MaryLou Roberts listed below.[7]

---

[4]Export.gov. 2014. "U.S.-EU Safe Harbor Overview, Overview," *Website.* https://2016. export.gov/safeharbor/eu/eg_main_018476.asp, (accessed October 13, 2019).

[5]General Data Protection Regulation (GDPR) Compliance Guidelines. (n.d.). https://gdpr.eu/, (accessed January 14, 2020).

[6]European Commission. "Fact sheet on the 'Right to be Forgotten' Ruling (C-131/12)," *PDF.* http://ec.europa.eu/justice/data-protection/files/factsheets/factsheet_ data_protection_en.pdf, (accessed October 13, 2019).

[7]M. L. Roberts (2019), "Impact of the GDPR after Almost a Year," https://im4thupdates.blogspot.com/2019/03/impact-of.html, (accessed March 3, 2020).

Companies need to carefully consider which aspects of the GDPR apply to them; there is not enough space in this short book to outline the impact of the new regulations on all firms. It is important to note the broad-reaching implications of the GDPR. California became the first state to pass data privacy rules similar to the GDPR with the California Consumer Privacy Act (CCPA), which became effective in January 2020. With so many states doing business with California, there are broad-reaching implications to the new act. In addition, many states are considering similar legislation and so many different laws could create a compliance nightmare for firms. The time is long overdue for the United States to have a consistent privacy policy on a national level. There are several pieces of proposed federal data privacy legislation and we all hope a solution may be forthcoming soon. Without national coordination, the burden of complying with rules from so many states will be burdensome and definitely will inhibit the free flow of commerce (see above) and company profitability.

Even with no national data privacy legislation in place, in the United States today, there are regulations regarding the privacy of PII as it relates to children under the age of 13 (Children's Online Privacy Protection Act, COPPA), the Gramm-Leach-Bliley Act for the disclosure of financial services data usage, and the Health Insurance Portability & Accountability Act (HIPPA) which gives patients greater control and access to health records. The United States has decided that in these three areas at least, some government regulation and control is necessary. Whether there will be more control in the future in the United States depends on the legislative process and the concerns of consumers in this area. The Internet Advertising Bureau (IAB) and other trade groups have also introduced principles for self-regulation of online advertising and tracking.[8] Consumers can look for an advertising icon which indicates compliance to get a sense if they wish to do business with a particular site. It is not likely that voluntary self-regulation will be the trend in the future.

---

[8]IAB. 2014. "Self-Regulatory Program for Online Behavioral Advertising," *Website*. https://www.iab.com/news/self-regulatory-program-for-online-behavioral-advertising/, (accessed October 13, 2019).

Security and Intellectual Property Issues

The issue of data security is related to data privacy because consumers often confuse the two concepts. It seems that hardly a month goes by without hearing about some type of data breach at a major company or a virus that has compromised our PII. In addition, the practices of phishing (e-mails attempting to collect PII), pharming (websites that look real but are not), and spoofing (imitating another person or site) are also threats to the integrity of our personal information. With more transactions being carried out online and over mobile networks that might not be secure, the danger to our information increases. Identity theft continues to rise and the bottom line is that fraud will continue to increase and we need to take steps to protect our information. Even the simple practice of changing passwords on accounts frequently can help protect our personal information.

This topic of legal issues in digital marketing, like the other chapter in this book, could each warrant their own book and chapter. I have tried to highlight the key issues in this area and would like to conclude with a word about intellectual property. The ability to share files digitally has impacted the world of intellectual property in a major way. The entire music industry, for example, has had to reinvent itself, albeit slowly, due to the appearance of file sharing services such as Napster. Although Napster had to take down its peer-to-peer (P2P) sharing system, only to re-emerge as a paid music downloading service, the lawsuits surrounding the service paved the way for an entirely new way of looking at the music industry.

Consumers today cannot only share content with each other but also receive music on the cloud, through music services, through streaming audio and video and the like. Rights management firms try to ensure that the creators of content receive credit for their work. The Digital Millennium Copyright Act (1998) was intended to protect authors and their publishers alike by ensuring that ISPs remove infringing content and that royalty fees are properly paid. However, with the ability to share information so easily on digital media, intellectual property rights, like data security and privacy, will continue to be a challenge. Some people advocate the Creative Commons approach, whereby authors can grant to the public some limited rights to their work.[9] I wonder if we won't go back to the systems popular before the modern era, where artists had sponsors to support them and did not rely on royalties for revenue.

What to Do Next after Chapter 8

1. Think about the particular campaigns or actions you recommended for your company or another firm for Chapters 4 through 7. What privacy concerns are related to these campaigns?
2. Based on your analysis in question 1, develop recommendations for the company to protect its customer data and still facilitate business.
3. Analyze the current legislation discussed in the chapter. Does any of this apply to the situation you selected? How does the legislation apply and how will you handle the legal issues in the business?

Discussion Questions

Discussion 8.1: Intellectual property as a concept is dead because of the Internet and digital communication. Do you agree or disagree and why?

Discussion 8.2: Discuss concerns that consumers may have about the privacy of their PII. What do you think a business can and should do to alleviate these concerns?

Discussion 8.3: Pick a company and read its privacy policy. What steps do you recommend the company use to further safeguard the personal information of its customers?

Discussion 8.4: Read Amazon.com's privacy policy as shown in the link above. What do you like about the policy? Is there anything that concerns you in the policy?

---

[9]Creative Commons. 2014. "About," *Website.* http://creativecommons.org/about, (accessed October 13, 2019).

Glossary

CCPA: California Consumer Privacy Act

COPPA: Children's Online Privacy Protection Act

EU Safe Harbor Provisions: Guidelines which companies had to follow regarding data to do business with firms in the European Union before the GDPR.

GDPR: General Data Protection Rules from the European Union that now regulate how data must be treated by firms doing business with EU companies.

HIPPA: Health Insurance Portability & Accountability Act

IAB: Internet Advertising Bureau

PII: Personally Identifiable Information

CHAPTER 9

The Customer Database, Analytics, and the Data-Driven Organization

Data Analysis Provides a Consistent Framework

In the beginning of this book, I said if it can be digitized, it can be measured. Without the customer database, digitized for access, we cannot perform marketing analytics. We might think of the types of analyses we wish to perform first, so that we make sure we collect the right data and have the right processes in place to clean that data. However, the database is the best place to start to develop an analytics program. In general, customer database includes internal, external, and modeled data (Figure 9.1).

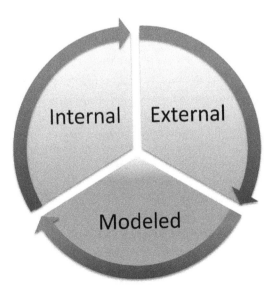

Figure 9.1 *Types of data that create the customer database*

Internal data (first party data)[1] is that data we collect about the customer. External data is what we purchase from elsewhere to "enhance" our database (third-party data) or obtain from a partner (second-party data) Modeled data is data that has been manipulated to include customer insights. Using the customer lifecycle from Figure 3.2 as a guide, we can determine what data we need at each stage of our customer lifecycle development process and collect and analyze data accordingly. When we are looking at a prospect, we may want to analyze website interactions and general demographic characteristics. When we are looking at an established customer, transaction history may be more relevant. Throughout this entire process it is important to uniquely identify the prospect or customer, typically using a unique customer identifier code. We need to identify customers to develop an effective messaging strategy and to interact with the customer most effectively.

For example, if the customer has recently left, we might need to understand their most recent purchase behavior. The company Screwfix, a UK distributor of power tools, identified its lapsed customers and tested various offers and subject lines in an e-mail "winback" campaign that had an 85 percent higher conversion rate than a standard e-mail from the company. The e-mails showed knowledge of past purchases from the company database, but used different messages to get the customer to purchase again.[2] For long-standing customers, we want to focus on the entire relationship and deliver offers of value. Hilton Worldwide, for example, tracks its customers in detail, knowing their preferences down to the type of pillow preferred. This data is used to provide superior customer service, resulting in extremely high customer loyalty.[3]

---

[1]Stirista blog (2020). "Third-Party Data: What it is, its Benefits and Best Use Case," https://www.stirista.com/blogs/third-party-data (accessed March 3, 2020)

[2]Young. 2014. "Relighting the Flame, Tested Email Strategies to Win-back," *DMA Case Studies*. http://www.slideshare.net/dmaemail/email-customer-lifecycle-2011-win-back-case-study-screwfix, (accessed October 13, 2019).

[3]Loyalty360. 2017. "Hilton Aims to Become the Most Customer-centric Loyalty Program in the Industry." https://loyalty360.org/content-gallery/daily-news/hilton-aims-to-become-the-most-customer-centric-lo, (accessed October 13, 2019).

Designing a Database Structure

Given the importance of customer data in marketing efforts, it is useful to consider at a high level the type of database to construct to store customer data. Companies frequently store unique customer identifying codes and other customer information in a single customer database, often using what is known as a data warehouse to store all their data in a single repository. The two broad categories of databases to consider when thinking in terms of reference and retrieval of relevant data are hierarchical and relational databases.

Hierarchical databases are built around a single, central record. All information relative to an individual customer is contained therein. There is no need in such a system to cross-refer to other data sources. Airline and hotel reservation systems have been developed in this way. Although hierarchical databases provide high-volume access and ease of use, their analytical capabilities can be limited by the extent of the data available. These databases are also known as transactional databases and are suitable for online-transaction processing (OLTP). Data input and data maintenance are easy, but reports and queries are more difficult.

Relational databases are a more recent approach to database development and utilization. They provide the advantages of simplicity and flexibility, minimizing redundancy and are more suited to ad hoc reporting. Typically, relational tables can be linked for reporting purposes. Related information is drawn from different, independent database sources as needed. A product database can be linked to a customer name/address database to direct promotion to specific product buyers. The separate product file enables analysis of a product line regardless of customer. Links can be established, too, with billing and/or shipping and inventory records.

How a Relational Database Is Built

A customer table can be built by using database software such as Microsoft Access. This database management system is one of many applications that allows creation, modification, and access via other applications for record manipulation. A data dictionary contains descriptions of the data within the database and allows flexibility in layout and formatting of files. Data is stored in tables having rows and columns linked together with a common key, such as a unique customer ID number. One column in a table could represent a customer name and each row an individual customer. Another column could contain the unique customer number that would allow a reporting system to link this table to another table that contains historical transaction data by customer number. Yet another table could be linked with information pertaining to the promotional efforts to that customer. Typically, a primary key of customer number links a "parent" table with a "child" table. This unique field will not contain duplicate values and can link one table to another in a one-to-many relationship. It is one-to-many because each customer can relate to many orders or promotional efforts.

One simple way to start is to use the Database Wizard in Microsoft Access to build a contact management system with predefined templates. The wizard leads the user through a series of design steps that provide several functions, including the ability to add optional and suggested fields, select a screen display, select a report style, and enter a title or name for a new database. Once the application is complete, the user can enter and modify data and develop new tables that link to keys within the customer file in order to expand the use of the database. Other cloud-based systems can also manage contacts effectively.

Relational databases are especially useful in tracking customer data because they have the flexibility needed to track this data, which often changes frequently. Relational databases offer the most flexibility in working with customer data as information to track may change frequently. Because of the table-driven features, relational technology is also more scalable and portable.

Beyond Relational Database Processing: OLAP and HADOOP

As database processing needs have increased, other forms of storing and accessing data have developed. For example, online-analytical processing (OLAP) stores data not in a table but in a "cube" or multidimensional format and enables the user to select data from different points of view. OLAP software can display all products sold to a particular customer segment at a certain price over a particular time period quite easily because of how the data is stored.

Apache Hadoop is an open source program that allows for the processing of all sorts of data, e-mails, web files, videos, and pictures. More importantly, the data does not have to be defined in terms of structure before it is accessed as in other database formats. Also, Hadoop allows for efficient processing of large amounts of data, such as the information created from large-scale website transactions or Twitter feeds. You will hear more about Hadoop and similar programs as the trend toward "Big Data" analysis continues. Real-time data processing to meet customer needs is another growing trend. Using data modeling techniques and artificial intelligence in real time, companies can present the right offer at the right time to customers and prospects, anticipating their needs rather than reacting to them.

What to Put in the Database

Regardless of the technical specifications involved, the most critical portion of database development is to decide what types of data to include in the database. The exact records to include is based on the type of company and its strategic goals and what information it needs to create its segmentation scheme and determine its most profitable customers. Basically, a customer database involves three sections. Figure 9.1 shows the three major aspects of a customer database: internal, external, and modeled data.

The three data types are described with examples in the Exhibit 9.1 below:

Exhibit 9.1
Internal, External, and Modeled Data are the Foundations of the Database

Internal data	External (Enhanced) data	Modeled (Analytical) data
(a) Agent and salesperson reports	(g) Compiled lists from outside data vendors	(l) Recency, frequency, and monetary value (RFM) scoring
(b) Customer financial reports	(h) Credit reporting databases	(m) Output from analytical models
(c) Web transactions and other inquiries	(i) Respondents to direct offers/web purchasers	(n) Customer profiling
(d) Social media traffic, where identifiable	(j) Industrial data for business purchasers	
(e) Post-sale requests	(k) Commercial segmentation schemes	
(f) Sales promotions		

Internal versus External Data

Although internal data comes from just where the name indicates—the company's internal records—and includes typically transactions data, what was purchased and when, and responses to sales promotions, it can also include data collected from the web and from interactions with salespersons and customer representatives (See Exhibit 9.2). External data providers abound and will be covered in more detail in a later chapter; the types of data most of interest to companies include credit reporting, lists compiled from other sources, and commercial segmentation schemes (segmentation based on multiple records and used to create categories of customers) such as those from Acxiom, Experian, or AC Nielsen (See Exhibit 9.3).

Modeled Data and Profiling

The modeled data in a database is developed from the internal and external data that the firm has collected or purchased and then uses to develop its marketing plans and strategies. Modeled data often results from analytical or statistical procedures. A simple analytical procedure such as RFM analysis ill yield "scores" that then can be input into a database. These scores can also be developed based on models using other types of internal and external information. Scoring is linked to the concept of profiling in that we seek out the best customers in our database and can develop a model that creates a score associated with our best customers (1 to 10, for example, with 1 being highest). Other types of modeled data based on the predictive techniques discussed in Chapter 9 can also help us identify and target our best customers and provide insight into marketing persona development. The model does not need to be based on RFM (recency, frequency, and monetary value) but can also be adapted to incorporate fields such as capacity to buy or other characteristics.

Exhibit 9.2
An Array Characterizing Types of Internal Information: Consumer

(a)	Age	(h)	Family composition
(b)	Gender	(i)	Street address
(c)	Income	(j)	E-mail address
(d)	Marital status	(k)	Length of residence
(e)	Race/ethnicity	(l)	Size of household
(f)	Education	(m)	Type of housing
(g)	Occupation	(n)	Web usage

Market Segmentation for Consumer Markets

Internal customer information for consumer databases can vary depending upon how much information is collected from the customer at the time of purchase or after the purchase. If the information is not obtained from internal sources, external sources will have to be used to augment or enhance the data. The exhibit above gives an example of some information that might be held in a customer database. This data can be used for market segmentation. Unlike a persona, a fictionalized description of the likely customer for the product, which includes a rich description of behaviors and preferences. A market segment is a homogenous subgroup of a heterogeneous aggregate market that is selected as a target market. Segments are often created out of database characteristics. Cluster analysis, for example, is an analytical technique for grouping of smaller entities, such as ZIP code areas or comparable individuals, into a market segment. Database marketing was the term for a group of techniques that eventually evolved into data analytics. Using a database wisely enables a marketer to target and focus on increasingly well-defined and profitable market segments. The process of segmentation (or market segmentation) begins with observing customers' actions and continues with learning about the demographic and psychographic (reflected in lifestyle) characteristics of these customers.

Market segmentation is a staple of marketing because it reflects a customer orientation and is facilitated by database information. It uses a rifle-shot approach that enables the marketer to target appeals to specific markets rather than a shotgun or scattershot approach that includes likely prospects but also includes many unlikely individuals. The most basic form of market segmentation is the division between ultimate consumers and business-to-business markets. But this segmentation is only the beginning. Brand preferences, product characteristics, potential purchase volume, price/cost, and recency and frequency of purchase are just a few additional ways of segmenting markets.

Segments should have similar characteristics and we should be reasonably assured that they will respond the same way to marketing actions. For example, segments of customers for a fast-food restaurant might be broken into groups of students/nonstudents and whether they live in the area or on campus or commute to campus. Over the years, some standard ways of segmenting markets have been developed. Consumer markets are segmented by geography, demographics, or psychographic (lifestyle) features that can be used to identify and to organize (or cluster) them into logical groupings using a variety of techniques. Commercial database firms such as Experian and Acxiom create various clusters of customers and segment them according to interests and stage of life in an attempt to make it easier for marketers to market relevant products.

Segmentation Based on Actions Taken

Direct marketers have used market segmentation based on actions taken as the traditional way to select responses or e-mail lists. The number of choices is nearly limitless, with consumer lists including buyers of all types of products, subscribers to specialized magazines, members of differentiated loyalty programs, donors to causes, collectors, and members. Lists of respondents are enhanced when there is an affinity, a relationship, a membership, or some form of expressed loyalty or connection to the organization.

These lists are enhanced, too, when divided into subgroups by characteristics of recency, frequency, and monetary value. For example, recent buyers ("hotline" buyers) of books about the Civil War are a segment within a segment (i.e., recent buyers of Civil War books as a segment of buyers of Civil War books). So are those who have been buying the annual update of an online directory for 10 or more years. So are those who buy "the best."

The number of segments and subsegments is limited only by the amount of data and the ability of the database manager to manipulate it. So, those who send gifts to others, as distinct from buying for their own consumption, comprise a segment within a segment. So are those who purchase as members of a select "club." So is the very large segment of "conscientious wheelers and dealers"—the millions of people who enter contests and sweepstakes, solve puzzles, buy lottery tickets, and order "genuine synthetic diamonds!" At heart, every mail or e-mail list represents a market segment that has demonstrated interest in certain offers by responding to them.

Exhibit 9.3
Types of External Information: Consumer

a. Geographic address
b. Telephone number
c. Gender of head of household
d. Length of residence
e. Number of adults at residence
f. Number of children at residence
g. Income
h. Occupation
i. Marital status
j. Make of automobiles owned
k. Transaction data such as purchase history
l. Salary level
m. Stage in purchase cycle
n. Key "events" in consumer's life
o. Ethnic and cultural considerations

Exhibit 9.4
Types of Internal Information: Business Customer

a. Transaction history
b. Purchasing address/contact
c. Shipping address/contact
d. Types of products/services purchased
e. Length of time as customer
f. Buying center/contacts
g. Stage in customer lifecycle/sales funnel

Exhibit 9.5
Types of External Information: Business Customer

a. Standard Industrial Classification (SIC) or North American Industrial Classification System (NAICS) code
b. Company size
c. Company revenue
d. Number of employees
e. Geographic location

Market Segmentation for Business Markets

In the United States, there are at least 10 times as many purchasing households (i.e., consumer purchasing entities or units) as there are B2B organizations, and about 25 times as many individual consumers. Not surprisingly, B2B information is different from B2C.

Although, information about an individual purchaser is similar whether the person is acting on his or her own behalf or that of an organization, it is obtained through a different set of segmenting tools.

Because the typical B2B buying decision is more complex than the typical consumer buying decision, targeted marketing has long played an important role in B2B marketing. For example, lead generation and qualification with digital technology are used extensively in B2B direct marketing to enhance the effectiveness of personal selling. Tools such as

Marketo, HubSpot, and Eloqua facilitate the lead nurturing and demand generation process in B2B firms, making the process of selling more cost-effective and eliminating the need for as many in-person sales calls. Digital technology such as search is also transforming the buying process, meaning the salesperson enters the process later in the sales cycle.

Direct contact in the form of sales calls to B2B buyers takes more time and is more costly than "calls" on consumers, which generally means that the consumer goes to the seller's place of business. B2B purchases typically involve much larger dollar amounts, and B2B buyers are usually much better informed, have more specialized interests, and are involved in a process of joint decision making with others in their organizations. Repeat purchases, too, are more frequent in industrial situations. These factors have combined to explain the need for, as well as the growing use of, market segmentation techniques described below in B2B direct marketing.

The Exhibit 9.4 shows that the company may have quite a bit of information about its business customers in its databases. Not only must a company understand an individual when it is marketing B2B but it must also understand who is involved in the purchase (the buying center). The customer lifecycle in the case of B2B can be particularly long, taking months and even years, so lead nurturing information must be collected and processed. Did someone at the company download a white paper or attend a webinar as a result of a content marketing campaign? This activity might bring them close to a purchase and must be noted in the database.

As illustrated above, there are five major data items that are generally used by B2B marketers to augment or enhance their internal data (See Exhibit 9.5). These items are SIC or NAICS code, company size, company revenue, number of employees, and geographic location. Beyond that, the information becomes quite specific to the industry. For example, companies selling computer software to be installed internally might want to know what operating system or systems the company was using.

Standard Industrial Classification Coding System

In the United States, the common means of external information used in industrial market segmentation is the SIC coding system developed and maintained by the federal government. This system is used to designate industry groups by function and product and, in a way, parallels the demographic characteristics used for segmenting markets and analyzing the demand of consumer markets. The first two digits of the four-digit code indicate major classifications of industry, of which there are often many subcategories.

The basic classifications of the two-digit SIC code are noted in the table below.

Two-digit SIC code	Industry classification
01–09	Agriculture, Forestry, and Fisheries
15–17	Construction
20–39	Manufacturing
40–49	Transportation, Communications, Public Utilities
50–51	Wholesale Trade
52–59	Retail Trade
60–67	Finance, Insurance, Real Estate
70–89	Services
91–97	Public Administration
99	Non-classifiable Establishments

The final two digits of the four-digit SIC code classify individual organizations by subgroup and further detail within industry. For example, SIC #2300 identifies manufacturers of wearing apparel. Within this classification, SIC #2311 identifies men's suit and coat manufacturers.

North American Industrial Classification System

SIC codes did a good job detailing the manufacturing industry in the post-World War II era, but many feel the system fails to recognize today's information technology age. With the rapid growth of the service industry, high technology, and international trade, a new system has arisen, largely in response to the North American Free Trade Agreement (NAFTA) of 1994. It was felt that a new system was needed to compare U.S. statistical information with that of Canada and Mexico. Desirable, too, would be future compatibility with an International Standard Industrial Classification System being developed by the United Nations. SIC codes are still used so are mentioned here.

However, all groups involved have agreed on a system, now called NAICS. This system has formulated a six-digit code, with the first five digits denoting the NAICS levels used by all three countries to produce compatible data. NAICS is an entirely different classification system focused on production activities rather than on the industries served, which is what SIC codes do. Different agencies within governments have converted to NAICS coding, but businesses have been slow to adopt the new coding system in marketing applications and SIC codes continue to be prominent.

Using Merge/Purge and Match Codes to Eliminate Duplication

In an earlier chapter, we spoke about the need to maintain data quality. A database must be designed to eliminate duplicated information and, thus, wasted effort. The more external lists are used to supplement a house list, the more complex this becomes. Lists are perishable. Customers move frequently and business professionals change jobs and job titles. Customer lists from different sources may duplicate each other; compiled lists may contain duplications *within, between,* and *among* lists; and many names may already be on a house list. The solution of using merge/purge and match codes eliminates duplication. Merge/purge can also be used to identify cross-channel behavior. Basic contact information must be constantly updated because of the mobility of both businesses and consumers. Transactions must also be kept up to date.

Organizing for the Data-Driven Organization

In summary, as companies put the customer database together, they look at internal, external, and modeled data to effectively create a complete view of the customer for analytical purposes. Although all types of data are important, there has been more of an emphasis lately on first-party data as various types of legislation impact how corporations manage and transfer data about their customers.

Although this chapter covers the technical details of the database, as discussed earlier, often the most important part of database marketing is how the organization is structured to handle the explosion of data that firms typically face. The term Big Data refers to databases which are so large that they cannot be handled by traditional data structures or data analysis methods. Big data analytics (BDA) "refers to the technologies and statistical techniques whereby marketers analyze large amounts of data to make useful inferences about customers and competitors."[4] However, most organizations need to worry about "Broad Data" or getting a 360-degree view of the customer from all areas of the organization. Typically, information is stored throughout the organization in older systems, known as legacy systems, which often makes it difficult to extract data for analysis.

Also, data is stored in many different databases which often don't speak to each other. These are known as data "silos" because the databases cannot easily communicate. A challenge is that the explosion in data from new sources such as Twitter feeds and website interactions, as well as video and other types of unstructured data, makes it difficult to look at a single view of the customer. As discussed previously, it takes good cooperation between marketing and IT, as well as general cooperation throughout the company, to manage data well. Key to an integrated company database is also top management support, including a vision for managing customer information that is made known throughout the organizations.[5] So database development, maintenance, and updates must be made an organizational priority.

Still, becoming a data-driven organization is not an easy task. In fact, a report by Experian states that in spite of recent emphasis on BDA, most companies (69 percent) struggle to become data-driven.[6] My coauthors and I believe that for an organization to be truly data-driven a number of steps are required in a process that includes sprouting, recognition, commitment, culture shift, and, finally, data-driven marketing. Briefly, after a few initial pioneers bring focus to the benefits of data-driven marketing to

[4]D.S. Johnson, L. Muzellec, D. Sihi, and D. Zahay. 2019. "The Marketing Organization's Journey to Become Data-Driven," *Journal of Research in Interactive Marketing* 13, no. 2, pp. 162-178. doi:10.1108/JRIM-12-2018-0157.

[5]D. Zahay, J. Peltier, A. Krishen, and D. Schutlz. 2014. "Organizational Processes for B2B Services IMC Data Quality," *The Journal of Business and Industrial Marketing* 29, no. 1, pp. 63-74.

[6]Experian. n.d. "White Paper: Data Enablement, Building a Foundation of Trust and Governance in a Data-Driven Era." (accessed September 23, 2019).

an organization, it takes a commitment throughout the entire organization and an integrated data platform to make the organization data-driven.

Where Do Analytics Fit?

Data-driven organizations are then able to take true advantage of analytics techniques in decision making. Segmentation, integrating third-party data in decision making, and predictive analytics are then available to the organization to enhance and inform its marketing efforts. Analytics itself is a broad term that means gaining insight from data. Most tools on the Internet have some form of analytics attached to them. If you set up a Facebook page or a YouTube channel, you will get some degree of data analysis to help guide your processes. You will typically be able to see how many people visited the site, where they came from, if they are new versus returning customers, how long they stayed, and the like. Analytics can be used to measure what goes on during a website visit or to explain both offline and online customer behavior. An easy way to get some ideas about analytics is to create a blogger blog and link that blog to Google Analytics so you can get a little practice. The steps are under the admin tab in Google Analytics. You first add a web property and then copy and paste the UA code number (i.e., UA-1237877-46) into the settings (other) section of your blogger blog. Soon you will be able to see the traffic sources to your blog, how long they stayed, and other useful metrics.

One form of analytics is **data analytics**. In this chapter, we have focused on setting up a customer database to develop any kind of analytics application. Although we can analyze market research or other types of data derived from outside the firm, we are primarily analyzing the company's internal data, augmented with external information and the results of our internal models. This data can be supplemented with website data and data from social media sites to get a true picture of the customer. With data analytics we look at the customer database and make insights. We might do an RFM analysis or look at our data in other ways to determine who the best customers are and how to market to them (Figure 9.2).

Data analytics can be descriptive but its greatest value to the company is in the predictive aspect. Therefore, we sometimes see the term **predictive analytics** mentioned online and in job descriptions in conjunction

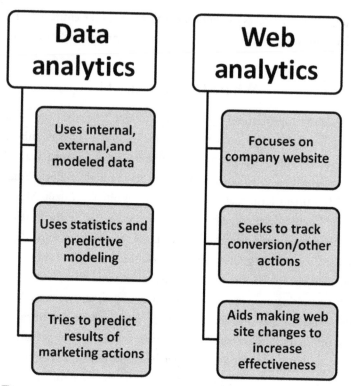

Figure 9.2 The two types of marketing analytics

with data analytics. This type of data is referred to as modeled data above and RFM is a simple example of modeled data in marketing. We try to use information about customer purchase patterns, such as how recently, how frequently, and how much was purchased, to predict future patterns and identify potential "best" or "high-value" customers. Predictive analytics often include regression or logistic regression models. Logistic regression predicts a 0/1 or binary-dependent variable and is very useful in marketing. Did the user buy or not? Is this someone to whom I should extend credit? There are many other binary logistic regression examples in marketing. There are many other examples in the marketing world.

Logistic regression is used to model data that does not follow a standard linear pattern where the data move in a one-to-one relationship. In linear regression, the effect of the predicted variable by a one-unit increase in the predictor variable stays the same. In logistic regression, the data follows a nonlinear fashion and the effects are different along the curve. (Charlotte Mason's 2003 note, *Applied Logistic Regression*, is available upon request for a more detailed explanation. Karl L. Wuensch's note, *Binary Logistic Regression with SPSS*, 2014, is also useful.)[7] More advanced techniques are also being explored and implemented to model customer response and are increasingly being implemented in real time.

You might be more familiar with **web analytics** such as the analysis provided by Google Analytics or similar programs. Web analytics, although it can use predictive models, often involve measuring the activity to a company's website with the objective of improving the flow of the site and meeting the company's objectives. In some web analytics, analysis is routine, and some are more exciting in nature as Justin Cutroni and Adam Singer from Google say in an Analytics Academy Live video.[8] Reporting is necessary and it is helpful if we can automate the process. Dashboards put information in one place to help marketers make a decision. Visualizations create a "picture" out of the data and also facilitate decision making. Dashboards, visualizations, and custom reports can help standardize information and make it easier to manage the business. You will always want to select your analytics goals based on your business objectives.

You will have set goals for your website from a business point of view and will want to track those goals that are important. If you want to increase traffic to the site, you can track the number of visitors. If you want to see if people clicked on a particular link, you can measure that. Typically measuring "conversion," the action you would like the consumer to take, in its various forms means doing some extra programming in whatever tool you are using. A conversion is usually linked to some kind of "call to action" or "desired action" taken by the customer. A while back Google Analytics changed and now has little information on the keyword source—how people search for your site. This information

---

[7]Wuencsh. 2014. "Binary Logistic Regression with SPSS," *Note.* http://core.ecu.edu/psyc/wuenschk/MV/Multreg/Logistic-SPSS.PDF, (accessed October 13, 2019).

[8]Google. 2014. "Analytics Academy Live with Justin Cutroni & Adam Singer," *Google Analytics Academy.* https://www.youtube.com/watch?v=cNr9QrzpEy8, (accessed October 13, 2019).

is available on a limited basis in the Google Search Console tool or (of course) if you are running a paid search campaign in Ads.

There are dashboards in Google Analytics which are essentially standard reports that help to see from which platform users are visiting the site, how long they stayed, and their country or region of origin. If you want to get more sophisticated conversion reporting in Google Analytics or any other analytics tool, you need to do something called "tag management." Using tags, or bits of code, on the website, you can then track conversions and other actions customers are taking. You can see how they moved through the site and where you might need to make corrections in the site to improve the customer experience. Tag management tools help marketers manage tags without having to go to the IT department for every change, thereby facilitating real-time changes based on customer response.

Google Analytics has a Solutions Gallery where various tools such as dashboards and custom reports are shared so you don't have to build reports from scratch. This repository is helpful because analytics are getting more challenging as customers are on multiple channels. E-mail marketing tools have analytics built into them but often we can't see how the customer is responding across channels. Measuring and allocating response across channels is called attribution modeling, and many analytics tools are trying to pull this information together. Analytics tools can attribute performance to the first "click" or interaction on a channel to the last "click" or interaction to try to determine which channels are most efficient and effective. Analytics as a discipline is getting more sophisticated, in general. If you take the Google Analytics training, you will see that we can analyze groups of users or site visitors. Segments are created on various characteristics, such as users with more than five transactions.

One of the most popular web analytics tools is Google Analytics, but there are other options that are well known, such as Adobe's Marketing Cloud and IBM's Analytics solutions. The idea is to get an idea of where the traffic is coming from in your website and who is converting and how, so you can make better marketing decisions.

Most analytics applications are set up in terms of dimensions and metrics. Not all dimensions have associated metrics. A dimension might be the type of user and a metric might be the total number of users in a period. Usually, we want to measure the result of some typical action and improve our marketing efforts. The analytics available without special coding (called tags) in Google Analytics include the type of browser being used and where the traffic originates, the time spent on the site, and the bounce rate (how long before the typical viewer leaves the site). As mentioned above, in most cases, you will need to enlist the aid of a developer to get the fine-tuned type of information needed for most marketing analysis, particularly e-commerce.

The most important thing from a management point of view is to think about what you really want to measure. For example, Google Analytics will tell you what country or region your traffic is coming from, but if you are primarily a domestic business, you may not care about that information. One final note is that, as with everything else, real-time analytics is set to become more and more important in the future as customers demand offers and answers when they are making their purchase decisions. Mobile analytics will also play an increasingly important role as most of our customer interactions will be on mobile devices.

The Customer Data Platform

A newer term in the world of customer data management is the customer data platform (CDP). The customer data platform can be seen as a software that integrates data from various sources for the purposes of analysis. HubSpot says a CDP is a software that aggregates and organizes customer data across a variety of touchpoints and is used by other software, systems, and marketing efforts. CDPs collect and structure real-time data into individual, centralized customer profiles.[9] It is hoped that this type of software can finally give companies that elusive 360-degree view of the customer in one platform alluded to earlier. The goals of the CDP include eliminating the problems with data "silos," that is, data being in several places in the organization at once with no integration. Whereas a CRM also tracks interactions, it does not function as a single place to create a customer profile from all interactions. Therefore, it appears that

---

[9]Decker. 2019. "What's a Customer Data Platform? The Ultimate Guide to CDPs." https://blog.hubspot.com/service/customer-data-platform-guide, (accessed January 14, 2020).

eventually the CDP will have impact on analytics in terms of being able to track multichannel interactions more effectively and help organizations on their path to becoming data-driven.

What to Do Next after Chapter 9

1. Make a list of the three types of data, internal, external, and modeled. Then rate which data your company or a company you select has most easily available.
2. Based on the campaigns and actions you said you might like to develop for Chapters 4 through 7, which type of data would most easily support these campaigns? Make a matrix of the campaign and the type of data needed and analyze the deficiencies you may have. What types of data do you need to further support these campaigns?
3. What would you hope to learn from both data analytics and web analytics to manage these campaigns and actions?

Discussion Questions

Discussion 9.1: Of internal, external, and modeled data in a customer database, which is the most important to marketing efforts and why? How do the three types of data work together?

Discussion 9.2: RFM is a long-standing type of modeled data. Why has it been so popular and how can the technique be adapted to your company or a company of your choosing?

Discussion 9.3: What are the top segmentation techniques for B2C and B2B customers? Give an example of the usage of these types of segmentation from your own or another company.

Discussion 9.4: What are the two main types of marketing analytics and how can they each be used to gain customer insight?

Glossary

360-degree view of the customer: Being able to track the customer's activity across all channels.

Big Data Analytics (BDA): Technologies and techniques to analyze large amounts of data to make useful inferences about customers and competitors.

Customer Data Platform (CDP): Software that integrates data from various sources for the purposes of customer analysis.

Dashboards: Putting information in one place to help make a decision.

Data analytics: Focusing on the customer database to gain customer insight.

External data: Data that the company purchases from a third party to enhance its customer database.

Former customers: Those that are no longer active purchasers.

Internal data: Data that a company collects as part of the customer life-cycle and doing business with that customer.

Match code: Abbreviated information about a customer record that is constructed so that each individual record can be matched, pair-wise, with each other record.

Merge/purge: A computerized process used to identify and delete duplicate names/addresses within house lists.

Modeled data: Data that is created as part of a "scoring" or other model to classify customer propensity to purchase or other characteristics.

Multi-buyers: An individual's name/address that appears on two or more response lists simultaneously.

New customers: Those who have made an initial purchase of a product or service. Often, the early behavior of customers is predictive of future behavior. Regardless, once acquired, the focus shifts toward encouraging repeat purchases and customer loyalty.

Predictive analytics: A form of data analytics that uses statistical or other techniques to predict customer response.

Prospects: Those in the target market, but who are not yet customers.

Recency/Frequency/Monetary (RFM): An assessment of the date, number, and volume of purchases; in the master list record over a period of time marketers can determine the transaction record of each customer in a given period, which helps determine the future potential of that customer.

Responders: Those who have made some contact with the business, but are not yet customers.

Retained or repeat customers: Customers who have made more than the initial purchase. Over time, customers can be characterized according to their value to the firm.

Visualizations: Creating a "picture" out of the data which also facilitates decision making.

Web analytics: Focusing on website logs and activity to gain customer insight.

CHAPTER 10

Managing the Digital Marketing Enterprise in a World of Marketing Automation

The Rise of Artificial Intelligence and Automation in Marketing

In applications powered by artificial intelligence (AI), a machine is programmed to make decisions on its own based on a set of rules and also to "learn" from the results of its decisions. In marketing, for example, ad placements through programmatic advertising and search engine marketing have increasingly lent themselves to automation. Using AI, machines make decisions about what you should be seeing to help you make decisions about products.[1] Most advertising on web and mobile sites is now programmatic, using algorithms to match the ad to the prospect or customer at the right time and place to maximize investment. In addition, currently about 20 percent of content served online is powered by AI and this figure is expected to grow to about 80 percent. AI also powers personalization and the web/mobile experience.

Automation in marketing can therefore be seen as both a blessing and a curse. The curse is that many individuals are worried that their jobs will be automated and taken over by AI applications and/or robots. However, the blessings of automation are both a better customer experience and

---

[1]Karlson. 2017. "8 Ways Intelligent Marketers Use Artificial Intelligence." https://contentmarketinginstitute.com/2017/08/marketers-use-artificial-intelligence/, (accessed January 16, 2020).

that the more routine tasks of marketing can be performed automatically, freeing up the marketer's time. Far from eliminating jobs, many thought leaders believe there will be more need than ever for marketers who can think strategically about digital marketing. In fact, less than two percent of respondents to the August 2019 CMO Survey[2] thought that technologies would replace marketing employees "a great deal" in the next year and less than three percent in the next three years.

Therefore, there will be more need than ever for those who know how to plan, implement, and measure a marketing campaign and link the marketing campaign to both the marketing strategy and goals of the organization and its broader mission and vision and strategic goals (Figure 10.1). We have discussed linking campaign goals to strategy elsewhere in this book. The rest of the chapter will focus on structuring and staffing the digital marketing organization in a world of agile marketing, AI, and an ever-expanding marketing technology stack.

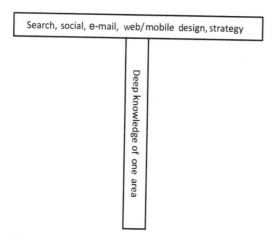

Figure 10.1 The "T" shaped digital marketer

The Marketing Technology Stack

The marketing technology stack refers to the tools and software that marketers put together to manage their marketing activities. These include tools such as marketing automation, content marketing, automated

---

[2]M. Christine. CMO Survey 2019.

advertising platforms, social listening, and analytics tools. It is estimated that there are over 7,000 (7040 to be exact as of this writing) tools to manage marketing in organizations, up from just 350 in 2012.[3] I strongly recommend you look at the link below to get an idea of the current landscape. One look at the dizzying array of technology choices is enough to make a digital marketer lose their mind and their patience. Marketers wonder how to effectively manage all these software and technologies and still achieve their objectives.

Because of the strong need for marketers to know about marketing technologies and techniques, it often is suggested that the digital marketer have a "T-shaped" background, which means not only an understanding of the various aspects of digital marketing but a deep understanding of one area, such as search, social, or analytics.[4] These T-shaped individuals in a digital marketing organization might have expertise in areas such as social media, content management, web/mobile design, marketing technology, digital strategy, and other topics discussed in this book as relevant to digital marketing. Indeed, there are many job opportunities for those with deep technical expertise as well as an overall knowledge of how their expertise works in the organization. Those individuals should be skilled in project management techniques such as agile marketing.

Agile marketing focuses on creating short-term goals and constantly revising them, allowing for more flexibility in responding to market conditions in the fast-paced world of digital marketing. Some marketing tasks that are suitable to agile marketing might include an A/B testing e-mail campaign, creating and testing web/mobile content, or overseeing advertising content.[5] While agile marketing has the benefit of developing flexibility in marketing organizations so they can better respond to market conditions, it is not the only capability required.

[3]Brinker. 2019. "Marketing Technology Landscape Supergraphic (2019): Martech 5000 (actually 7,040)." https://chiefmartec.com/2019/04/marketing-technology-landscape-supergraphic-2019/, (accessed January 15, 2020).

[4]De Baere. 2016. "The CMO's Guide to Digital Marketing Organization Structures." http://www.b2bmarketingexperiences.com/2016/04/cmos-guide-digital-marketing-organization-structures/, (accessed January 16, 2020).

[5]Rooney. 2014. "Applying Agile Methodology to Marketing Can Pay Dividends: Survey." https://www.forbes.com/sites/jenniferrooney/2014/04/15/applying-agile-methodology-to-marketing-can-pay-dividends-survey/#e37ac3b6acd0, (accessed January 16, 2020).

In digital marketing organizations today, individuals skilled in creating marketing dashboards, visualizations, and telling stories with data are also valued. There is no shortage of skills in demand, but digital marketers today also need a broader perspective.

These individuals skilled in dashboarding and visualization must also be able to link key performance indicators (KPIs) to overall goals and demonstrate how performance is measured in a way that can be easily explained throughout the organization.

Structuring the Digital Marketing Organization

The question then remains with such specialized skills: Should there be a separate digital "team" in the organization, or should digital skills be integrated into the organization? The general consensus appears to be that we still need to have marketers with specific digital marketing skills in the marketing organization. Many marketers today are still the lone digital specialists in their company, responsible for covering all the trends and tools we have discussed this book. Clearly, more support is needed for these individuals. Digital strategist Dave Chaffey believes that we still need digital teams within organizations, particularly in industries where the vast majority of the business is online.[6] He believes the best structure is a centralized digital team that provides support and training to digital specialists throughout the marketing organization. This type of structure avoids the pitfall of having a centralized digital team with others in the organization taking a "hands-off" approach.[7]

Within the digital marketing organization, there are numerous roles to be staffed. Chaffey suggests some key roles are a chief digital officer or digital transformation manager to help integrate digital throughout

---

[6]Chaffey. 2019. "10 reasons you still need a digital team." https://www.smartinsights.com/managing-digital-marketing/resourcing-digital-marketing/10-reasons-you-need-digital-team/, (accessed January 16, 2020).

[7]Hanlon. 2018. "Digital marketing team structure examples." https://www.smartinsights.com/managing-digital-marketing/managing-digital-transformation/maximising-digital-performance-effective-digital-transformation/, (accessed January 16, 2020).

the organization, as well as a digital marketing manager and a marketing technology manager to oversee day-to-day functions. Other essential roles would be managers for the topic areas we have discussed in this book, such as one expert each for organic and paid search, a content manager across platforms, an analytics expert, someone to test and manage and improve digital experiences (CX), a conversion rate optimization specialist, a CRM and e-mail marketing manager, and social media marketing executives. This organization structure in terms of scope and responsibilities is visualized in Figure 10.2, with some suggestions based on this text. For example, CX and CRM have been grouped together and marketing technology is a specific role coordinated by the digital marketing manager. Specific roles and responsibilities would be dependent upon the industry, the company structure, and the resources the company has to fill these roles. Some companies outsource specific roles to supplement internal expertise in digital marketing. In terms of the CX, Walmart combined its online and offline product-buying teams to try to facilitate more consistent pricing and a better customer experience. Expect more organizational decisions to be made with the customer experience in mind.[8]

I tend to agree with Chaffey that a digital marketing "expert" group is needed in organizations because of the technical expertise involved in so many aspects of digital marketing. It is also my opinion that spending time on structuring the digital marketing organization and constantly updating that structure based on changing market conditions can reap substantial benefits for firms. Often organizational structures are developed haphazardly and not while keeping a focus on reaching the customer better and improving their experience. In the case of both digital marketing strategy and organizational structure for digital marketing, a little planning goes a long way.

---

[8]Nassauer (2020). "Walmart to Combine Online and Store Product-Buying Teams", https://www.wsj.com/articles/walmart-to-combine-online-and-store-product-buying-teams-11582643932 (accessed March 2, 2020).

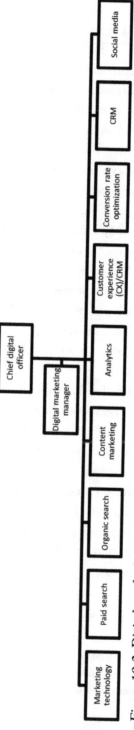

Figure 10.2 Digital marketing organization scope and responsibilities

What to Do Next after Chapter 10

1. Make a list of three technologies in the marketing technology stack that are most important for a particular business. Who in the organization knows those technologies best and can help train others?
2. Based on the campaigns and actions you said you might like to develop for Chapters 4 through 7, which type of organization structure would most easily support these campaigns? Make a matrix of the organizational structure, KPIs, campaign objectives and analyze the deficiencies the company may have. What types of organizational changes does the company need to make to further support these campaigns?
3. What should the company hope to learn from applying agile marketing to manage these campaigns and actions?

Discussion Questions

Discussion 10.1: Is automation and artificial intelligence in marketing more of a blessing or a curse?

Discussion 10.2: Has the marketing technology stack become unwieldy in terms of the many choices that abound? What are some solutions to streamlining the stack?

Discussion 10.3: Is there a need for a separate digital marketing organization within companies in this day and age?

Glossary

Agile marketing: Managing the marketing function by focusing short-term goals and constantly revising them.

Artificial Intelligence (AI): Where a machine is programmed to make decisions on its own based on a set of rules and also to "learn" from the results of its decisions.

KPIs: Key performance indicators for managing the organization.

Marketing technology stack: The tools and software that marketers put together to manage their marketing activities.

Programmatic advertising: Using algorithms to match the ad to the prospect or customer at the right time and place to maximize investment.

CHAPTER 11

Concluding Thoughts

This book has covered the major issues related to digital marketing today. Its premise has been the importance of understanding the process of digital marketing in a strategic context. Prior developments in marketing thought and terminology led to the development of digital marketing as a widely used term for using marketing technology to foster interactivity and engagement (see Figure 11.1). The company web/mobile site, e-mail, social media, and search strategies and marketing goals and objectives should all function together. This integration is difficult to accomplish if each functional area in the company is working on a different strategy. Certainly, education of managers and entry-level employees in this area is important, which is one of the purposes of this book. However, equally important from a management point of view is the education of the executive. It is hoped that the CEO and CMO can read this book and understand better how to move forward to create an organization not only digitally literate but as someone who can implement the company vision and strategy in this area. CMOs want to be more "data driven" than intuitive but don't always know how to get there.[1]

Maybe even this short book is a little overwhelming to some readers. It will help to do the exercises suggested at the end of each chapter. After doing them, you should be able to launch a more effective digital strategy in any type of firm. I would also suggest to the audience reading this book

---

[1] Marketing Charts staff. 2014. "US CMOs: Spending on Analytics, Social and Content Growing," Marketing Charts. https://www.marketingcharts.com/digital-44671, (accessed October 13, 2019).

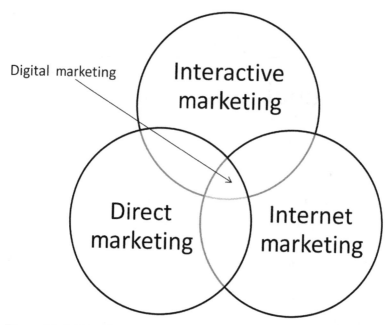

Digital marketing

Figure 11.1 Digital marketing incorporates the best aspects of prior terminology

that the most important aspects of creating an effective digital marketing strategy and managing that strategy effectively would be as follows:

1. **Create a clear company strategy around digital marketing and customer data excellence. Communicate that strategy throughout the entire organization.**

   The research shows that companies that can capitalize on customer information management and other types of digital strategies create a clear mission and vision and communicate that strategy throughout the entire organization. Using the House of Quality for multichannel marketing can help create strategies across channels and then measure across channels as best as you can.

2. **Start with your web/mobile and move outward.**

   The core web/mobile design is the key to managing digital marketing within the firm. The sites and landing pages to which you are driving your customers should convey the key message and be a landing destination for customer engagement efforts. Focus from there on the other elements of the digital marketing delivery mix.

3. **Develop metrics and key performance indicators (KPIs) around that strategy.**
What's the objective? Are you in prospecting mode, win-back mode, or trying to create deeper customer relationships? How will you measure success? Consider the customer lifecycle, the customer acquisition and relationship management continuum, and the basic objectives of attract, acquire, retain, and engage when setting objectives and measures.

4. **Reward middle managers and others responsible for implementation.**
If there is a disconnect between the company rewards systems and the digital strategy, then results won't be achieved. Implementation must also take place in customer-facing roles.

5. **Make it easy to share data in the organization.**
Data "silos" and a lack of data sharing make it difficult to share information and to achieve performance results.

6. **Encourage and reward the functional marketing area and their IT counterparts to work together.**
Teamwork comes from the corporate vision and setting a clear strategy. This teamwork in turn leads to digital marketing success. Don't rush into a digital strategy without the underlying structure for success. And don't overlook processes for data quality, as customer data quality leads to performance.

7. **Keep up to date.**
Take a look at the articles and websites cited in this book. Many times, my students follow the websites and companies recommended in the links in class. There are many good sources of data on digital marketing to keep current. This book provides a structure, but monitoring what is happening in the marketplace will help you stay current. Some of the newsletters I receive include those from Marketing Charts, eMarketer, and Search Engine Land. Dave Chaffey's Smart Insights website offers a wealth of information on digital marketing strategy and organization.

I wish you all good luck in your digital marketing efforts. Whether working in a growth environment, a global pandemic or a movement for social justice, the basic framework of this text remains relevant. We must deliver value on digital platforms based on data and analysis. Please do not hesitate to be in touch with any questions. Follow me on LinkedIn to continue the conversation at http://www.linkedin .com/in/drzahay. Instructors may request copies of Power Points and an instructor manual by e-mailing me at debra@zahay.com or debrazb22@gmail.com or through LinkedIn at http://www.linkedin .com/in/drzahay. The materials are also available on the BEP website (www.businessexpertpress.com). I am always happy to help.

APPENDIX

Digital Marketing

Plan Outline

Digital Marketing Plan Outline

Part I: Details of the company background.

1. **Title/Cover Slide:**
   - Company name, product/service name, date.

2. **Executive Summary:**
   - Key problems/issues that the marketing plan will solve. Describe the goals of the digital marketing plan.

3. **Company Analysis:**
   - Define the scope: corporate/organizational, SBU, or brand level, usually depending on the size of the organization.
   - Brief background on the business (products, services, target market, brand image).
   - Objectives/Mission statement.
   - Business model(s) currently used (how the company makes money).

4. **Current Marketing Situation Analysis:**
   - Market/industry analysis (size, growth, trends).
   - Value chain analysis: how the company delivers value currently.
   - Customer segmentation (customer base: demographics, psychographics, geographic).
   - Competitor analysis (existing competition, potential competitors, product substitutes).
   - Customer acquisition and relationship management objectives per Figure 1.8.
   - Customer lifecycle stage analysis and objectives per Figure 3.2.

- Channel relationship matrix (customer channel preferences, our channels): gap analysis (Figure 7.1).
- Channel correlation matrix (how customer channels currently work together) (Figure 7.1).
- Keyword analysis: how customers search for the product/service.
- Current positioning statement.

5. **SWOT Analysis:**
   - Business strengths.
   - Business weaknesses.
   - Business opportunities.
   - Business threats.

6. **Company's Current Digital Marketing Efforts:**
   - Four foundations of digital marketing delivery mix or DMDM (social, search, e-mail, web/mobile) integrated with core marketing strategies and objectives.
   - Customer service, acquisition, retention strategies.
   - Overall marketing strategy.
   - Integration of digital presence into overall marketing strategy.
   - Offline approaches.
   - Data acquisition, management, use, and structure.
   - Current performance, metrics, evaluation.
   - Social and regulatory issues.
   - Other relevant issues/topics.

Part II: Details of your digital marketing plan and how the company should implement it.

7. **Digital Marketing Objectives and Strategies:**
   - Define the scope: corporate/organizational, SBU, or brand level, usually depending on the size of the organization.
   - Describe how the marketing plan will contribute to helping the company achieve its business objectives.
   - Objectives/goals of the digital marketing plan.
   - Overview of intended digital marketing strategies.

8. **Action Plan—Detailed Suggestions You Would Like the Company to Follow, Including but Not Limited to:**
   - Business and revenue model(s) for your product or service.

- Target market: customer selection, segmentation, targeting.
- List of keywords that define the business to be deployed across channels.
- Positioning statement in the format of Chapter 2.
- Traditional four P's (product/service, pricing, distribution, promotional mix).
- Four foundations of digital marketing delivery mix integrated with marketing strategies (e.g., website, social media, e-mail, search, web/mobile).
- Online/offline integration of marketing communications plan including search, social, e-mail, and web design elements as well as relevant offline elements.
- Specific mobile/website strategy for product/service (design, features, functionality, usability).
- SoLoMo: How social, local, and mobile will work together.
- Integration of social media with content marketing strategy.
- Customer acquisition, conversion, retention, and engagement plans as appropriate based on the customer relationship management objectives in Figure 1.6, the customer lifecycle objectives in Figure 3.2, and the customer acquisition and relationship management process outlined in Figure 8.1.
- Channel relationship matrix (customer channel preferences, our channels) (Figure 7.1).
- Channel correlation matrix (how customer channels should work together) (Figure 7.1).
- Details on communications channel activities, that is, social and mass media and other online secondary channels.
- Distribution/fulfillment of marketing messages, material, incentives, and so on.
- Quality and customer service structure required to execute this plan.
- Technological infrastructure (marketing technology stack) and data requirements required to execute this plan.
- Managerial structure required to implement this plan. (See Figure 10.2).
- Social and regulatory issues.
- Other relevant issues/topics.

9. **Control/Feedback/Financial Analysis:**
   - Performance measurement: describe the metrics to be used to evaluate performance as relevant from each chapter.
   - Include customer lifetime value (CLV) and return on investment (ROI) objectives.
   - Match performance metrics precisely to marketing objectives.
   - Include Google Analytics and other web data.

About the Author

Dr. Debra Zahay is full professor of marketing and director of the Master of Science in digital marketing and analytics at St. Edward's University in Austin Texas. She holds her PhD from the University of Illinois, Urbana,-Champaign, her MBA from Northwestern University in Evanston, Illinois, her JD from Loyola University in Chicago, Illinois and her AB from Washington University in St. Louis, Missouri.

Dr. Zahay researches how firms use customer information for competitive advantage. She has published extensively and presented her work at many academic and practitioner conferences. She has co-authored two additional textbooks in digital and social media marketing.

Index

CPSIA information can be obtained
at www.ICGtesting.com
Printed in the USA
FSHW020503021020
74276FS